MW01701293

Bright Kids™ Spatial Visualization Workbook for the NNAT®2 – Levels A and B

Written and published by: Bright Kids Publications™

 ISBN 978-0-9855178-5-4.

Bright Kids Publications™
225 Broadway
Suite 1400
New York, NY 10007

Phone: 917-539-4575
Email: info@brightkidsnyc.com
www.brightkidsnyc.com

About Bright Kids NYC™

Bright Kids NYC™ was founded in New York City to provide language arts and math enrichment for young children. Our goal is to prepare students of all ages for standardized exams through assessments, tutoring, parent workshops, and our publications. Our philosophy is that, regardless of age, test taking is a skill that can be acquired and mastered through practice.

At Bright Kids NYC™, we strive to provide the best learning materials. Our publications are truly unique. All of our books have been created by qualified psychologists, learning specialists, teachers, and staff writers. Our books have also been tested by hundreds of children in our tutoring practice. Since children can make associations that many adults cannot, testing of materials by children is a critical step towards creating successful test preparation guides. Finally, our learning specialists, teaching staff, and writers have provided practical strategies and tips to help students compete successfully on standardized exams.

Feel free to contact us if you have any questions.

Corporate Headquarters
Bright Kids NYC™ Inc.
225 Broadway
Suite 1400
New York, New York 10007

Phone: 917-539-4575
Email: info@brightkidsnyc.com
www.brightkidsnyc.com

Introduction

Bright Kids Publications™ created the Spatial Visualization workbook for the NNAT®2 Levels A and B to familiarize students and parents with the Spatial Visualization questions on the NNAT®2. Students, no matter how bright they may be, do not always perform well if they are not accustomed to the types of questions found on a standardized exam. Thus, without adequate preparation and familiarization with the Spatial Visualization questions on the NNAT®2, a student may not perform to the best of his or her ability on the actual test.

The *Bright Kids™ Spatial Visualization Workbook for the NNAT®2 – Levels A and B* can help a student become accustomed to the Spatial Visualization questions found on the NNAT®2. This workbook contains 60 figural construction and deconstruction skill-builder exercises, 50 Spatial Visualization questions, and 20 advanced paper-folding exercises to help a student hone his or her visual-reasoning skills. The Spatial Visualization questions on the NNAT®2 are considered to be the most difficult question type on the exam. Thus, it is important for a student to become adept at solving these types of problems if he or she wishes to achieve a high score on the NNAT®2.

In order to maximize the effectiveness of the Bright Kids™ Spatial Visualization workbook for the NNAT®2 Levels A and B exams, you should familiarize yourself with the workbook, reviewing all of the exercises and practice questions. Once you are familiar with the workbook, it is recommended that you work with your child in a neutral environment free of noise and clutter. It is also important to work at a slow but consistent pace through the workbook with the child. Finally, a comfortable seating arrangement may help the child focus and concentrate to the best of his or her ability.

Most students will have to take numerous standardized exams throughout their school years. The best way to develop the critical-thinking skills for these types of exams is to practice with similarly-styled questions. This method helps ensure that a student will succeed on his or her exam.

NNAT®2 Overview

The *Naglieri Nonverbal Ability Test® - Second Edition* (NNAT®2) is designed to provide a nonverbal measure of a student's general cognitive ability. Students do not use their reading, writing, or speaking skills on the NNAT®2; instead, they must rely on visual reasoning and logic to solve the problems presented to them. Since the NNAT®2 is completely nonverbal, it can be used with diverse populations of students. The NNAT®2 is an updated version of the *Naglieri Nonverbal Ability Test® - Multilevel Form* (NNAT®-ML; Naglieri, 1997).

All of the information needed to solve each NNAT®2 problem is presented in the item. For example, one matrix format requires a student to identify what will happen when two or more figures are combined or deconstructed.

Figure 1: Sample NNAT®2 Question

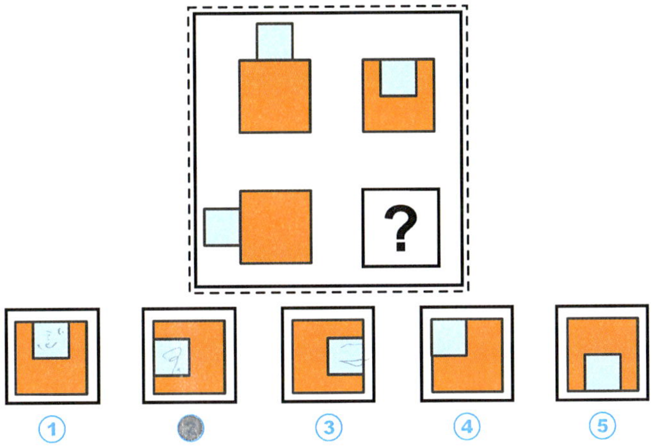

NNAT®2 scores provide an estimate of the student's cognitive ability in relation to other students of the same age. The NNAT®2 can be administered in a group or online.

The NNAT®2 is a timed test; students have 30 minutes to complete 48 questions.

NNAT®2 Content

The NNAT®2 is a nonverbal measure of general cognitive ability that is specifically designed to predict academic success. The student must examine the relationships among the parts of a matrix and determine the correct response based on the visual information provided within the matrix. A student must pick the correct response from five possible answer choices.

The NNAT®2 test consists of the following four question types:

1. Pattern Completion

The first question type requires a student to identify the correct piece that completes a visual pattern. These types of questions appear more on elementary level NNAT®2 tests since they are among the easiest of the matrix items.

Figure 2: Pattern Completion Example

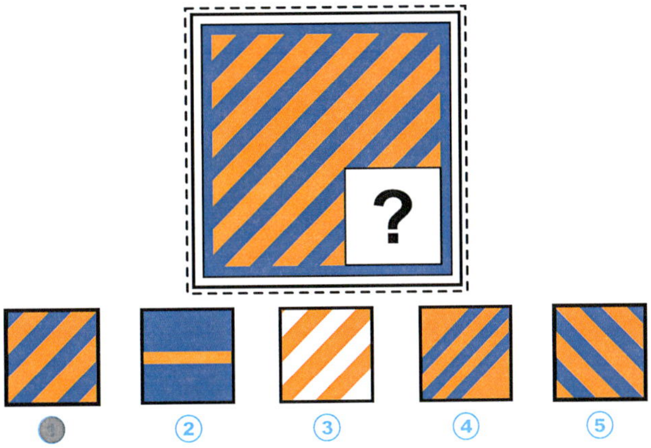

2. Reasoning by Analogy

The second question type requires a student to recognize a logical relationship between several geometric shapes to find the right answer. The student must notice how the objects in the boxes change as you move across the top row of the matrix. Then, he or she must apply the same relationship to the objects in the first box in the second row in order to determine the correct picture that belongs in place of the question mark. These items increase in difficulty when multiple changes occur across rows and columns.

Figure 3: Analogy Example

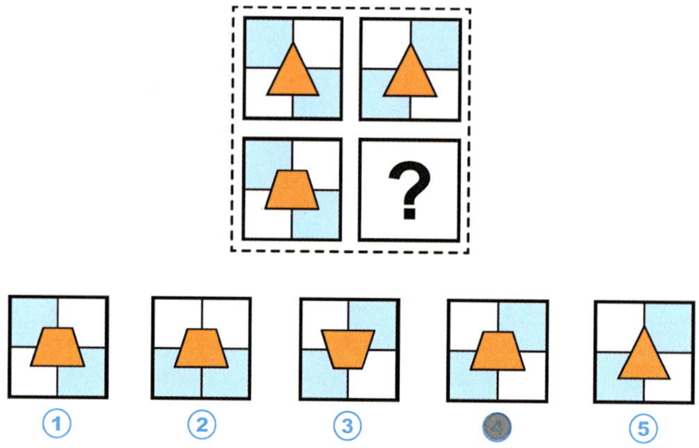

3. Serial Reasoning

The third question type requires a student to recognize a sequence of shapes and how the sequence changes across the rows and columns. This type of matrix becomes more difficult when multiple series are included in the matrix.

Figure 4: Series Example

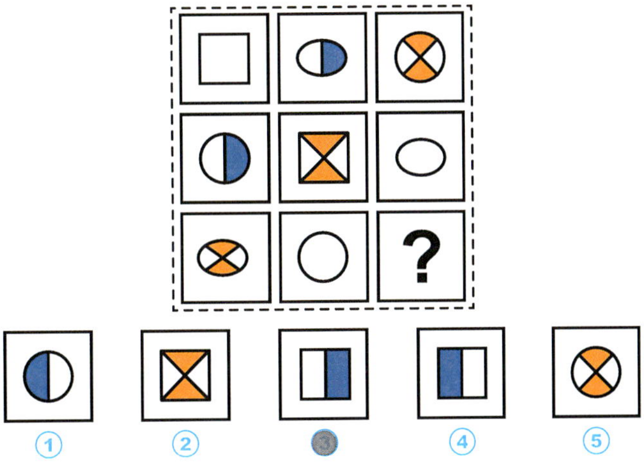

4. Spatial Visualization

The fourth question type requires a student to recognize how multiple designs would look if they were combined or deconstructed. The student must find the answer by examining the images in the boxes above and to the left of the empty box to determine what image belongs in place of the question mark. These types of questions are more complex since they involve shapes rotating or intersecting in ways that might be difficult to visualize.

Figure 5: Spatial Visualization Example

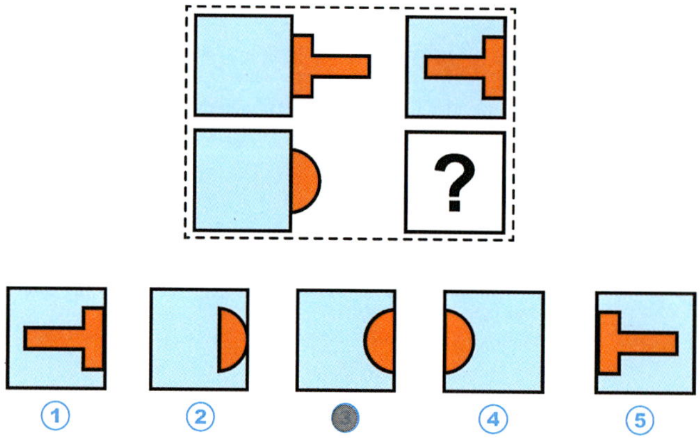

NNAT®2 Test Structure

The NNAT®2 is organized into seven levels, A through G, that are designed for students between kindergarten and twelfth grade. There are 48 questions on each level of the exam. Due to students' rapid cognitive development in earlier grades, there is a level for kindergarten, first, and second grade. There is one level that is for third and fourth grade and another level that is for fifth and sixth grade. The next level is appropriate for the middle school years and the transition to high school. The last level serves the last three high school grades (i.e. tenth, eleventh, and twelfth grade). See the table below for the summary of NNAT®2 test levels and their corresponding grades.

Table 1: Summary of NNAT®2 Levels and Grades

Level	Grade(s)
A	K
B	1
C	2
D	3, 4
E	5, 6
F	7, 8, 9
G	10, 11, 12

How to Use This Workbook

Spatial Visualization questions require a student to accurately predict how a set of designs will look when combined, deconstructed, or spatially "folded". This workbook starts with figural construction and deconstruction skill-builder exercises. For figural construction questions, two pieces of a puzzle are presented. The objective is to find what the completed puzzle will look like when both pieces of the puzzle are combined. For figural deconstruction questions, there is a figure at the beginning of the row that consists of two pieces placed together. Here, the objective is to identify the correct two pieces to the right that could be combined to make the same figure. These skill-builder exercises are included in the beginning of the workbook to help a child become accustomed to recognizing how shapes and figures can be combined or separated.

The Spatial Visualization questions on the NNAT®2 require a student to determine the correct answer by visualizing complex rotations or folds along an axis to a given shape or set of shapes. These types of questions tend to be among the more challenging on the exam because they involve rotations or shapes intersecting in ways that might be difficult to visualize. There are several ways to support your child when working through the Spatial Visualization questions in this workbook:

- Use activities like origami to help your child understand how to create three-dimensional shapes from plain paper. If your child can follow instructions and complete a design, then he or she will be able to understand how visual-spatial elements combine to create a new design.
- Students will also benefit from utilizing the process of elimination on this type of question. Children can take a long time to answer Spatial Visualization questions, so eliminating a few answers can avoid frustration and save time since the NNAT®2 is a timed test.

We have also included 20 paper-folding exercises in the back of this book as an additional challenge. For each question in this section, the student is shown a piece of paper that is being folded. Then, a hole is punched into the folded piece of paper. He or she will need to visualize what the paper will look like once it has been unfolded. These exercises will help strengthen your child's spatial-visualization skills.

Bright Kids™
Spatial Visualization Workbook for the NNAT®2

Levels A and B

Skill-Builder Activities:
Figural Construction and Deconstruction

Fill in the circle under the shape that is created when the first two shapes are combined.

01

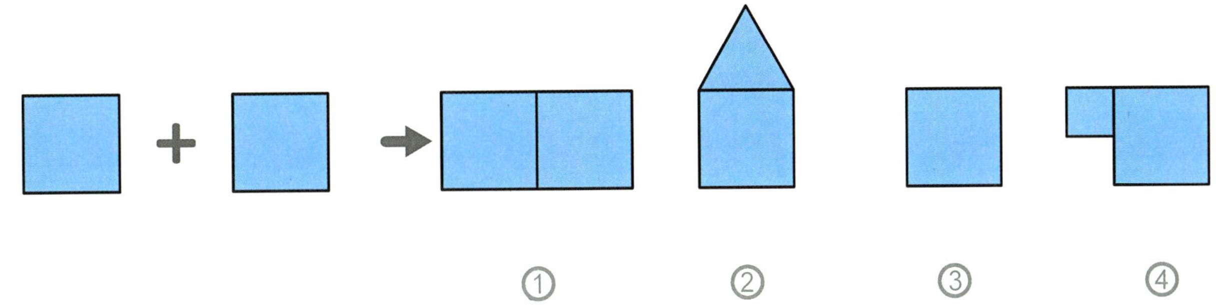

02

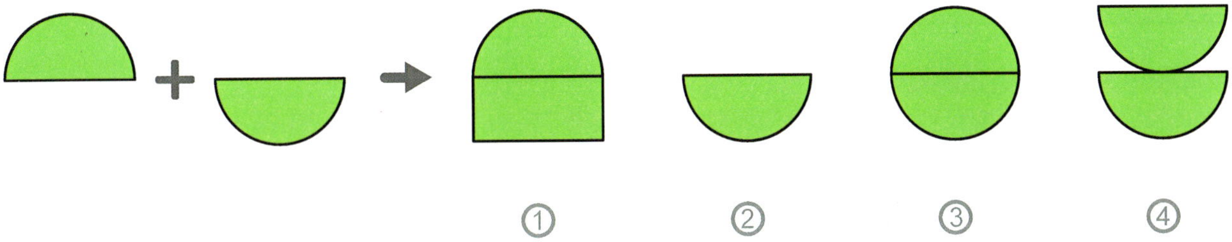

03

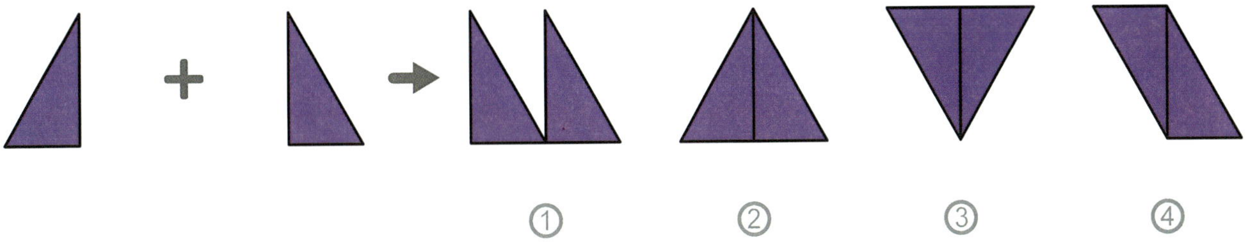

04

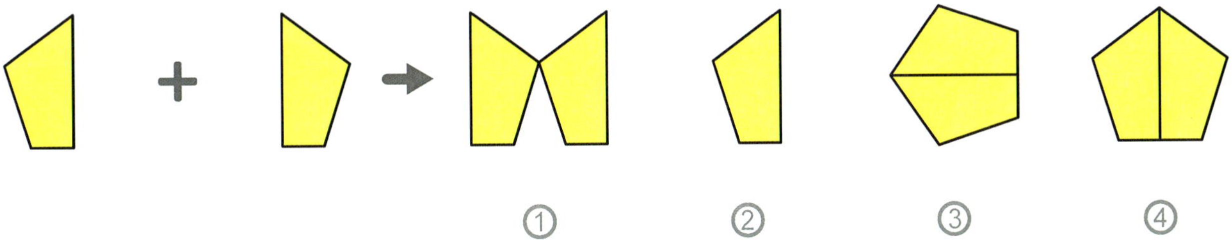

05

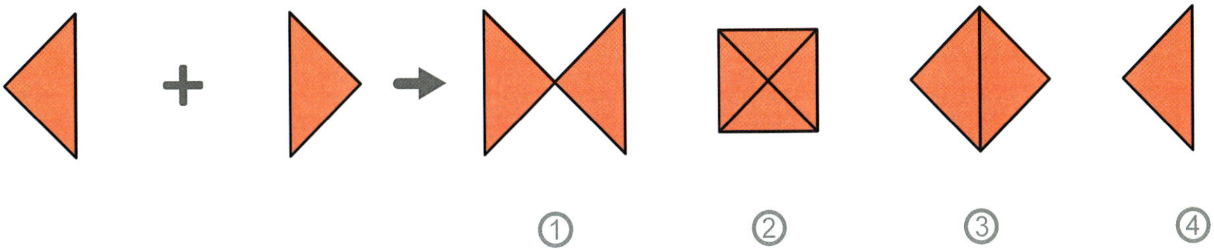

Fill in the circle under the shape that is created when the first two shapes are combined.

06

① ② ③ ④

07

① ② ③ ④

08

① ② ③ ④

09

① ② ③ ④

10

① ② ③ ④

Fill in the circle under the shape that is created when the first two shapes are combined.

11

① ② ③ ④

12

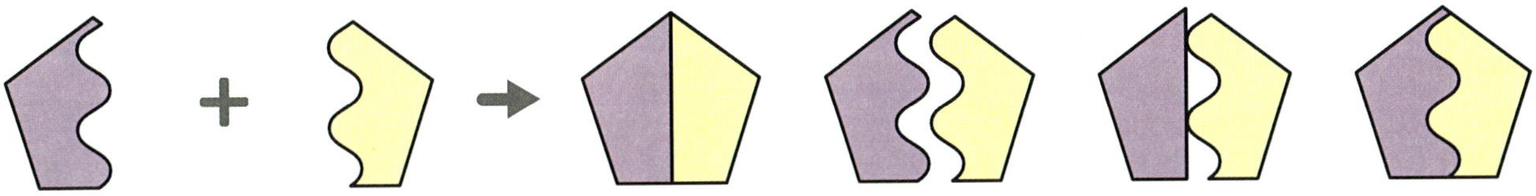

① ② ③ ④

13

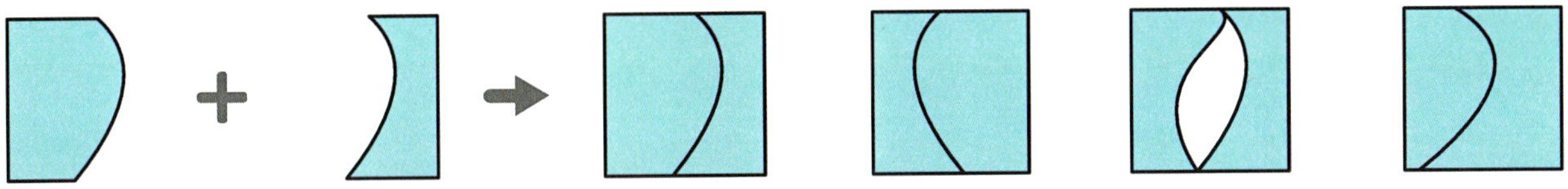

① ② ③ ④

14

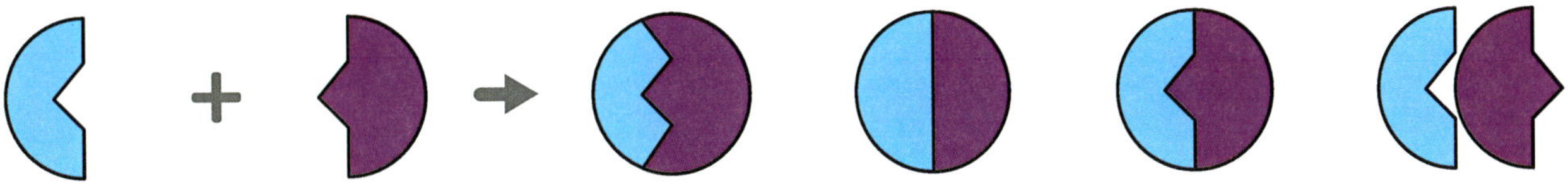

① ② ③ ④

15

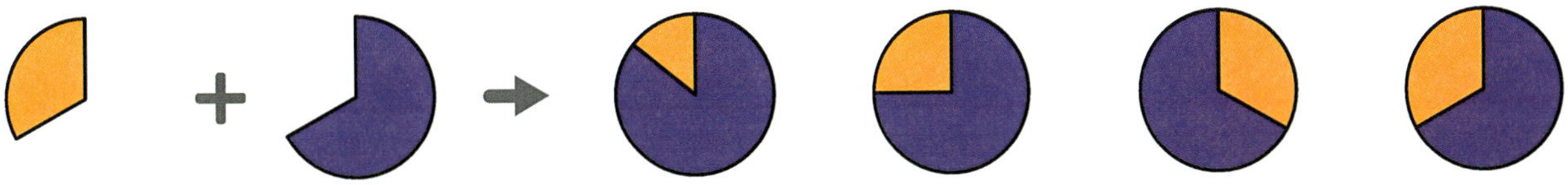

① ② ③ ④

Fill in the circle under the shape that is created when the first two shapes are combined.

16

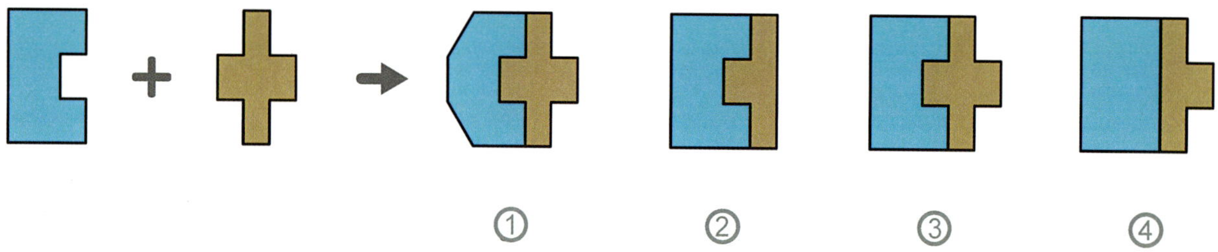

17

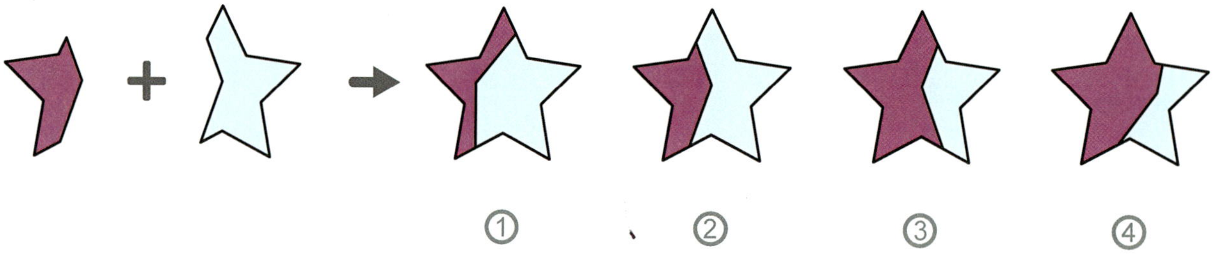

18

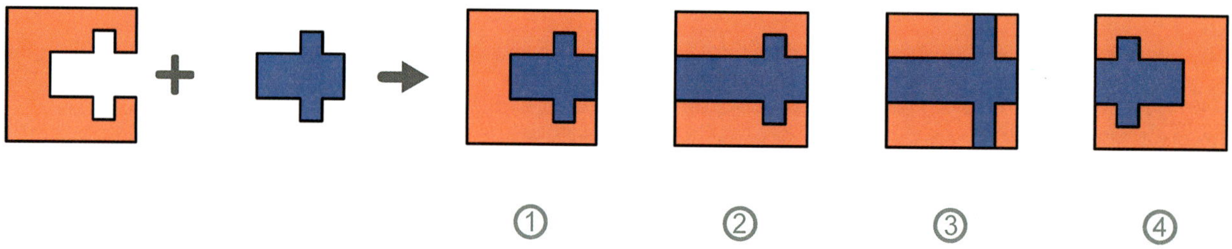

19

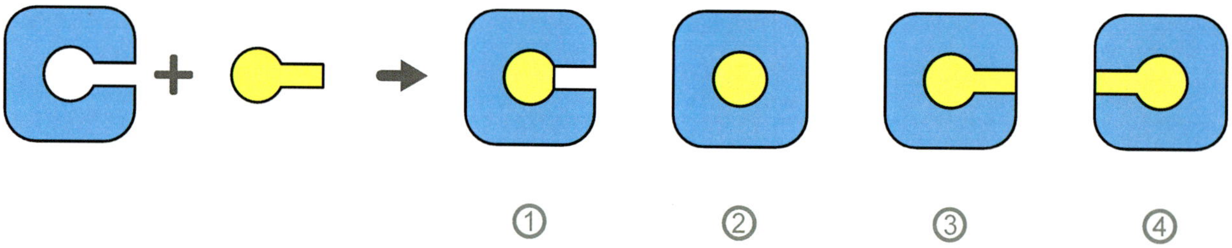

20

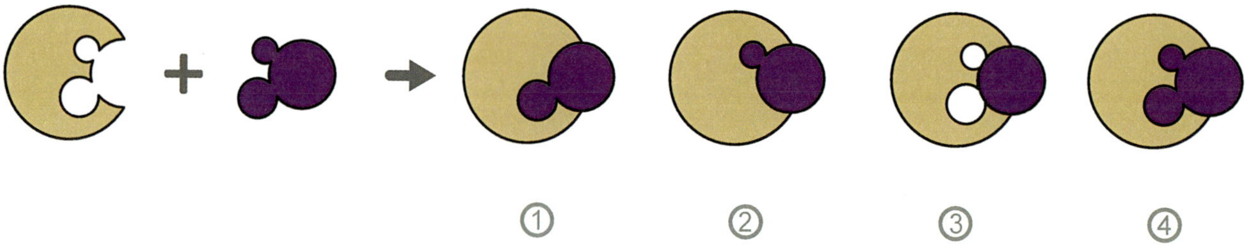

Fill in the circle under the shape that is created when the first two shapes are combined.

21

① ② ③ ④

22

① ② ③ ④

23

① ② ③ ④

24

① ② ③ ④

25

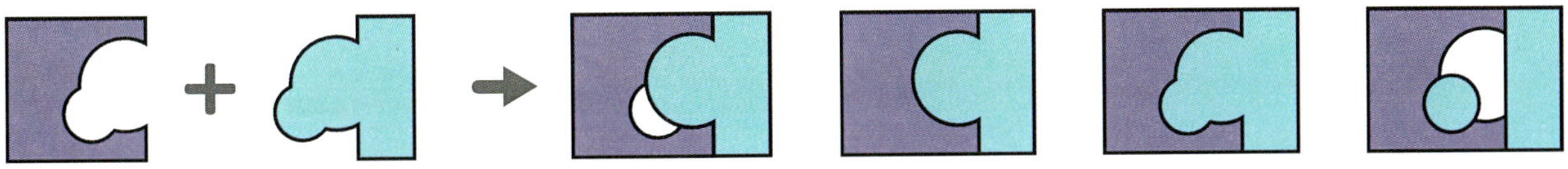

① ② ③ ④

Fill in the circle under the shape that is created when the first two shapes are combined.

26

① ② ③ ④

27

① ② ③ ④

28

① ② ③ ④

29

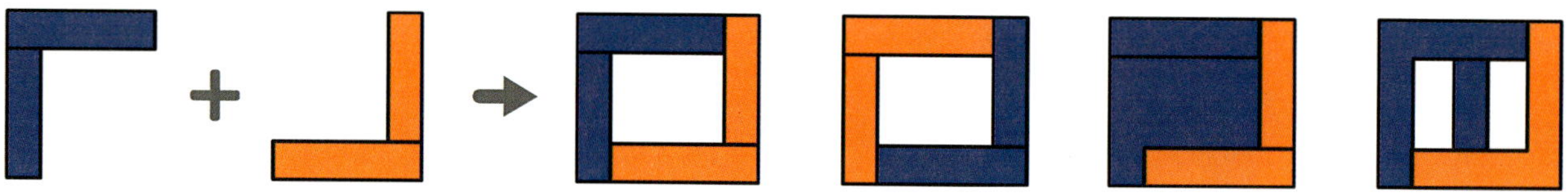

① ② ③ ④

30

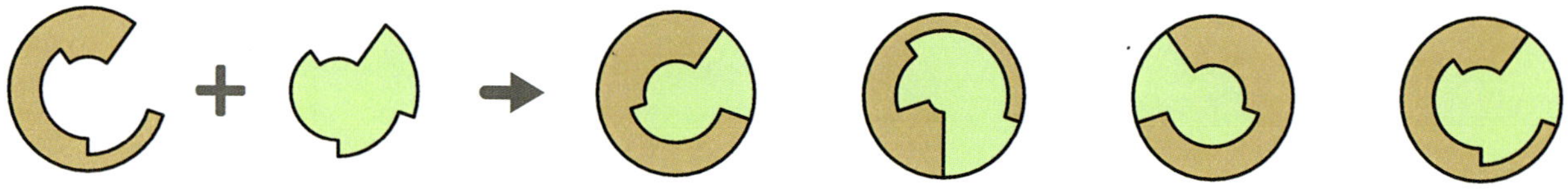

① ② ③ ④

Fill in the circles under the two pieces that would make the shape on the left.

01

① ② ③ ④

02

① ② ③ ④

03

① ② ③ ④

04

① ② ③ ④

05

① ② ③ ④

Fill in the circles under the two pieces that would make the shape on the left.

06

① ② ③ ④

07

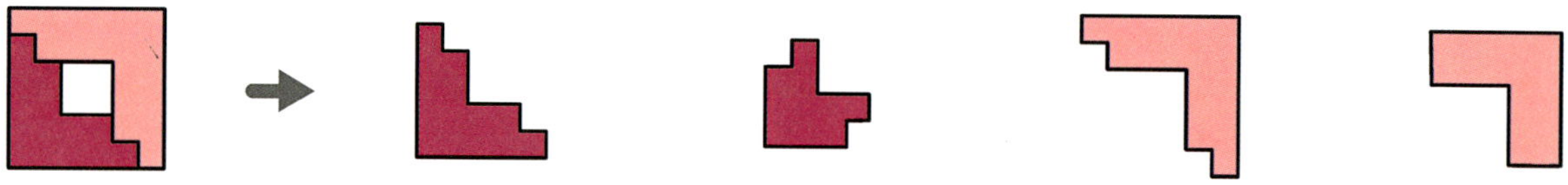

① ② ③ ④

08

① ② ③ ④

09

① ② ③ ④

10

① ② ③ ④

Fill in the circles under the two pieces that would make the shape on the left.

11

12

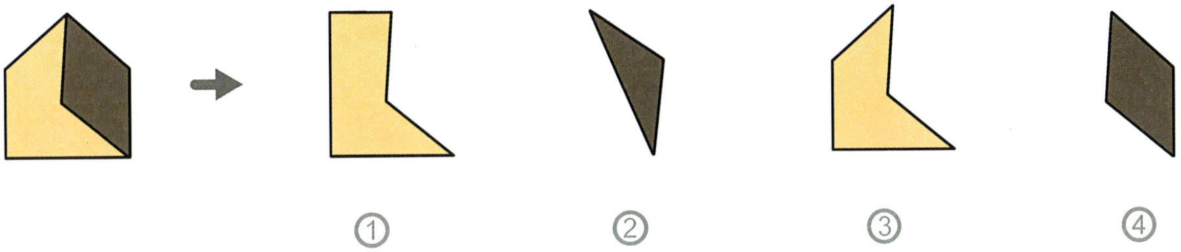

13

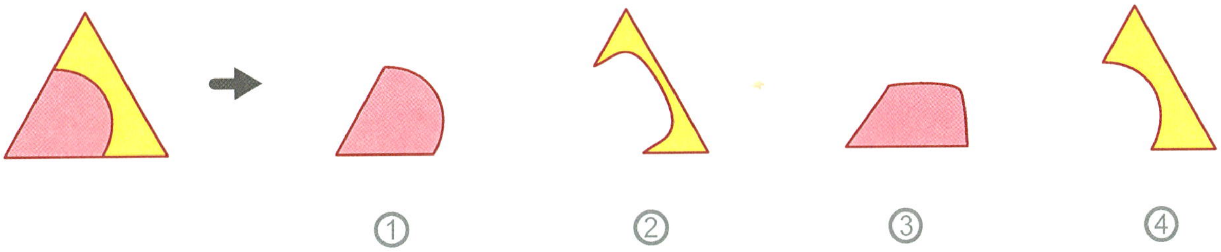

14

15

Fill in the circles under the two pieces that would make the shape on the left.

16

① ② ③ ④

17

① ② ③ ④

18

① ② ③ ④

19

① ② ③ ④

20

① ② ③ ④

Fill in the circles under the two pieces that would make the shape on the left.

21

① ② ③ ④

22

① ② ③ ④

23

① ② ③ ④

24

① ② ③ ④

25

① ② ③ ④

Fill in the circles under the two pieces that would make the shape on the left.

26

① ② ③ ④

27

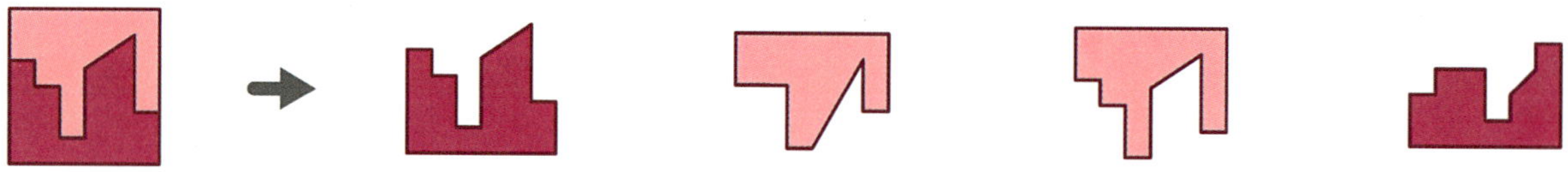

① ② ③ ④

28

① ② ③ ④

29

① ② ③ ④

30

① ② ③ ④

Bright Kids™

Spatial Visualization Workbook for the NNAT®2

Levels A and B

Spatial Visualization Questions

Sample Questions Administration

SAY: **Today, we are going to do some fun activities. We will do the first two activities together.**

Sample One

SAY: **Look at the picture below. There is something missing. Look at the answers below and find the piece that is missing.**

S1

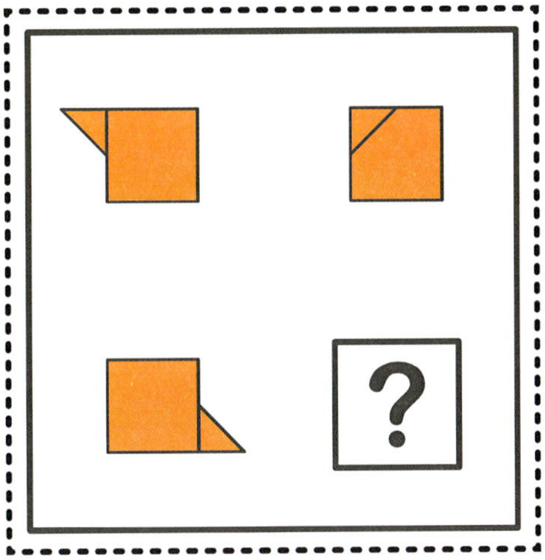

SAY: **Yes, the piece should be the box with the triangle in the bottom right corner, which is number 2. Fill in the bubble with the number "2" inside it. This is the correct answer.**

Demonstrate how to fill in the answer if the student seems confused. Remind him or her that a bubble must be visibly filled in for the question to be properly scored. Also let the student know that he or she can bubble in only one answer choice. Answer the student's questions and make sure that he or she is comfortable with the answer choice.

Sample Two

SAY: **Look at the picture below. There is something missing. Look at the answers below and find the piece that is missing.**

S2

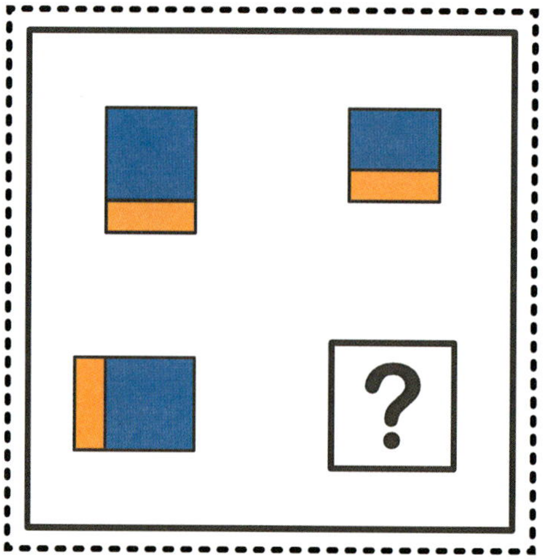

SAY: **Yes, the piece should be the blue box with the orange rectangle on the left side, which is number 1. Fill in the bubble with the number "1" inside it. This is the correct answer.**

Answer the child's questions and make sure that he or she is comfortable with the answer choice.

SAY: **On the next few pages, you will be doing more activities like these. Do the best that you can with each picture and do not worry if you are not sure of all of the answers. Be sure to bubble in the whole answer space each time you mark your answer. If you want to change an answer, erase all of your first mark and mark the new answer.**

01

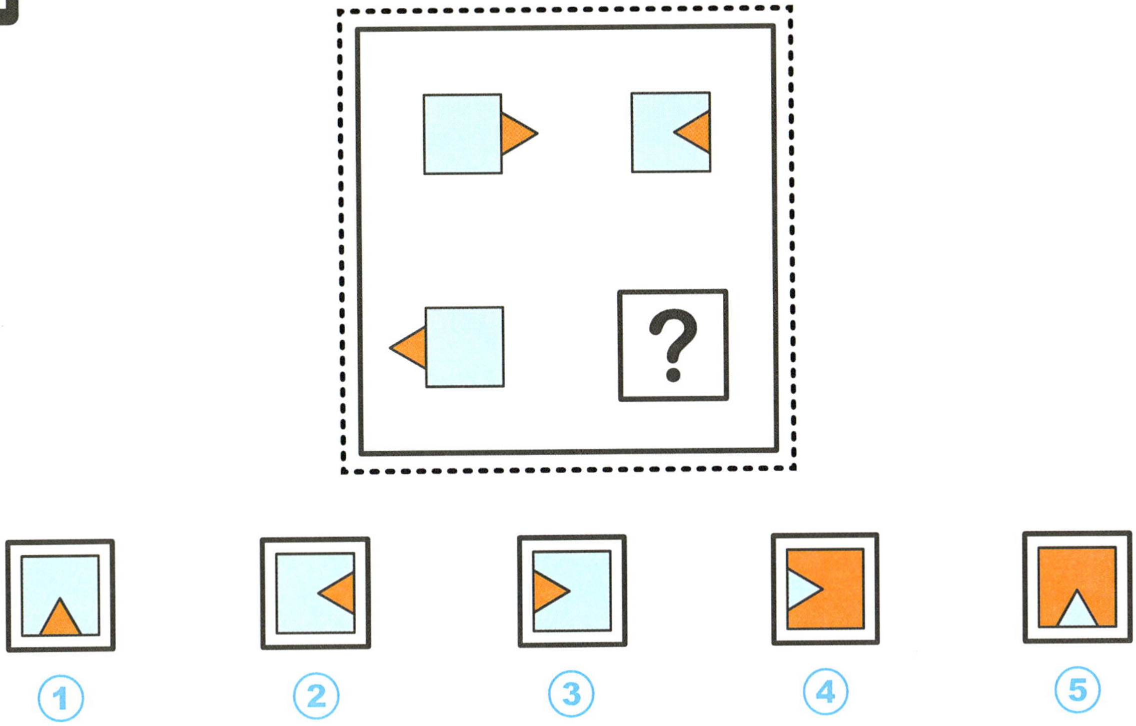

02

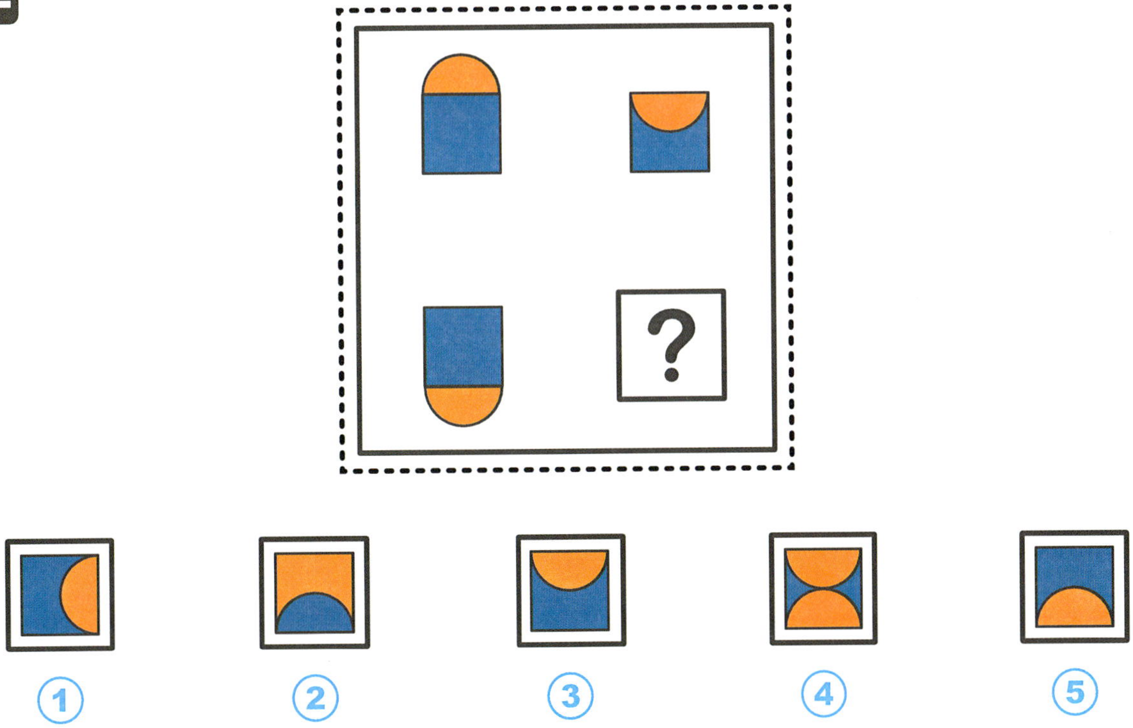

03

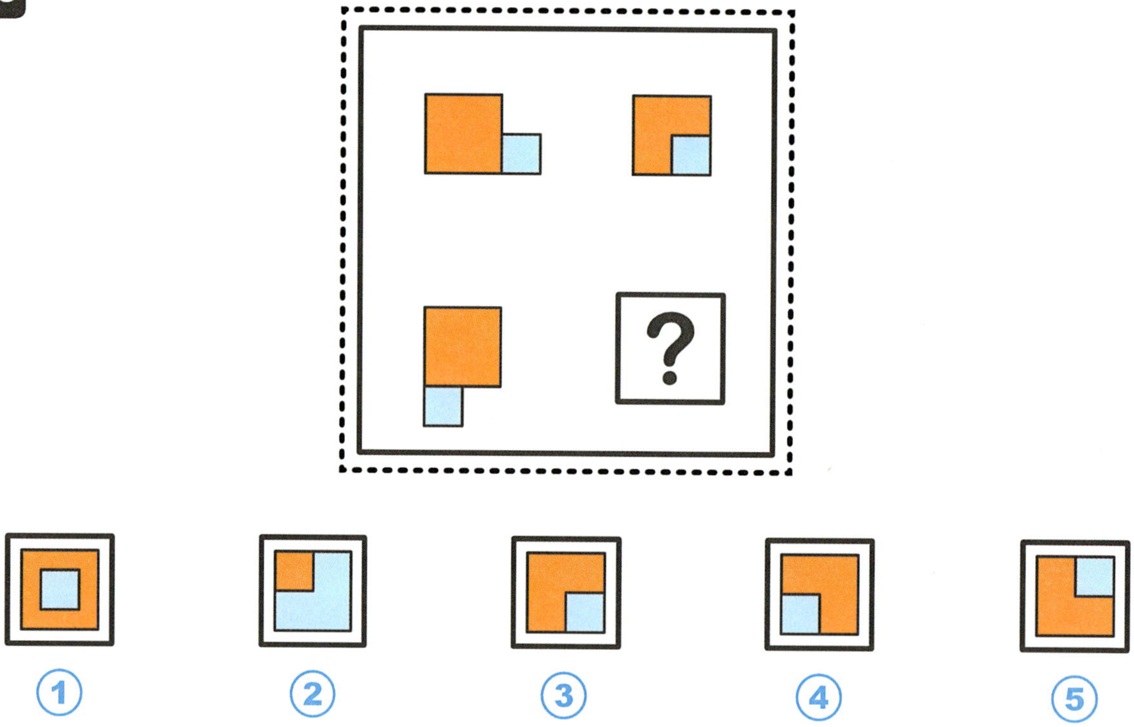

04

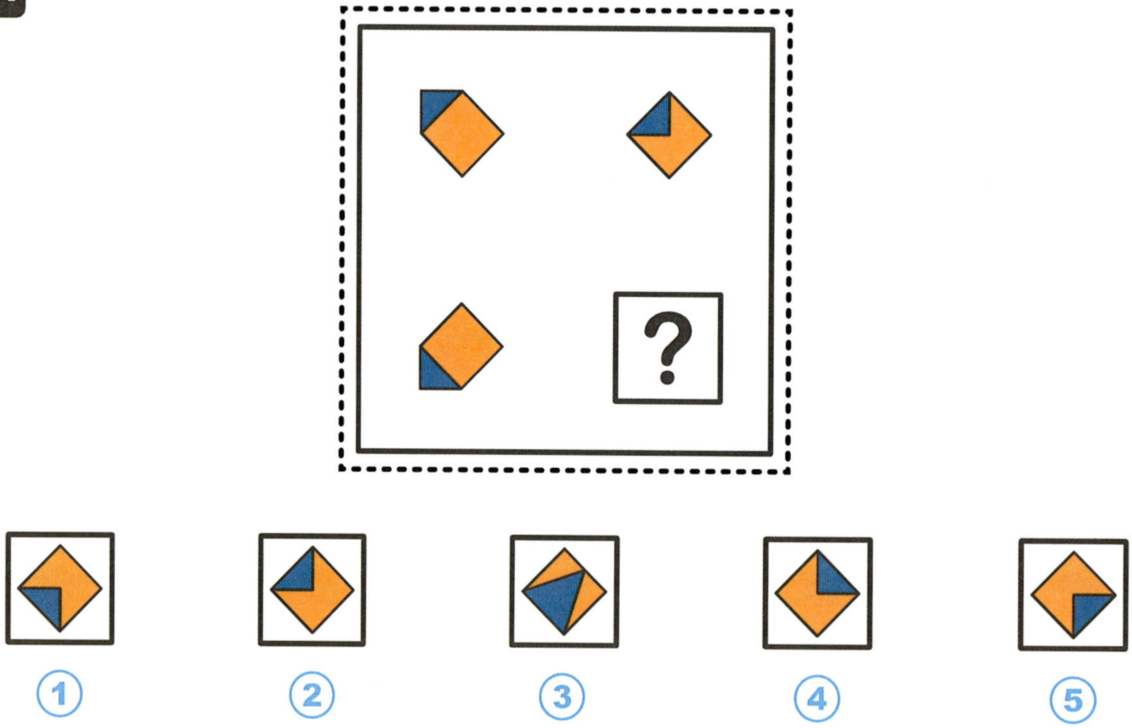

05

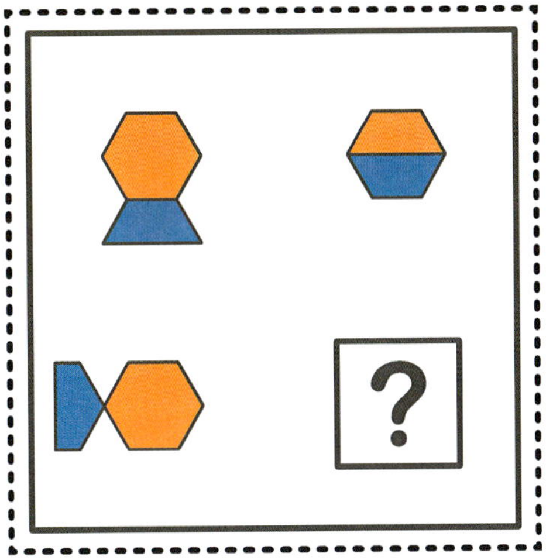

1 2 3 4 5

06

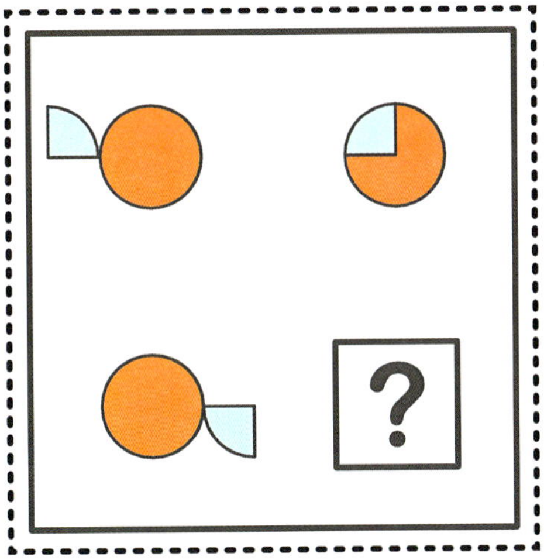

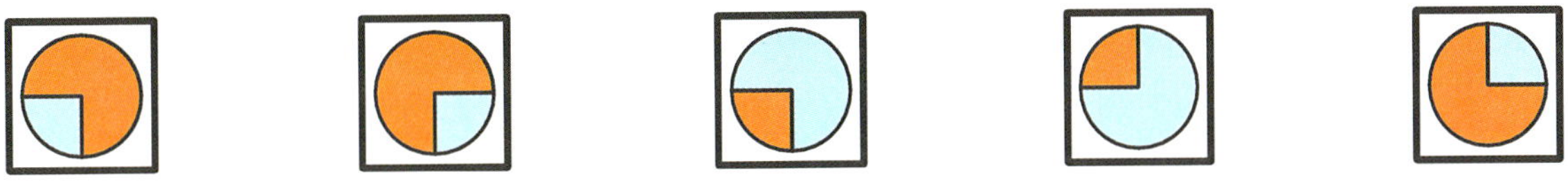

1 2 3 4 5

07

08

09

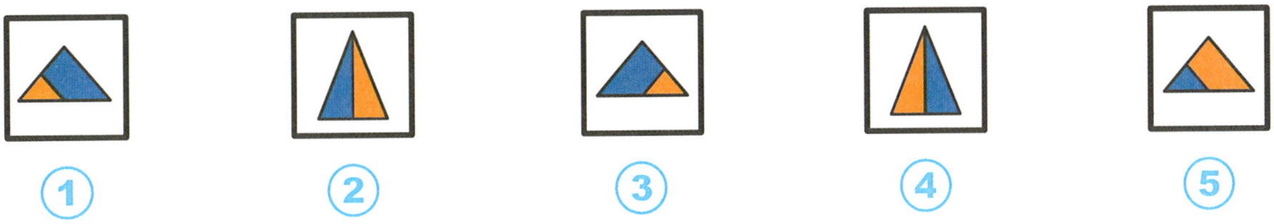

10

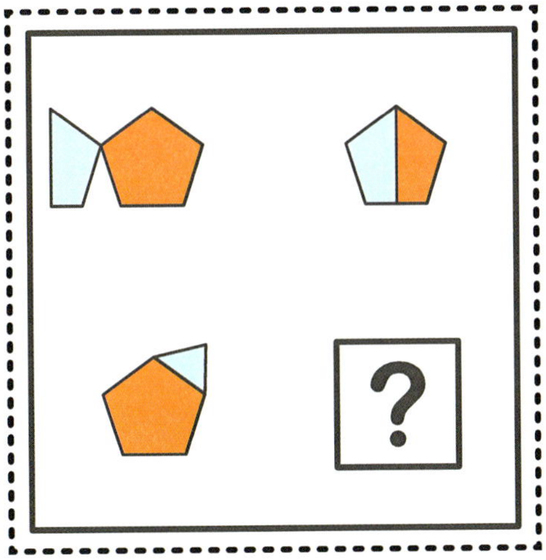

11

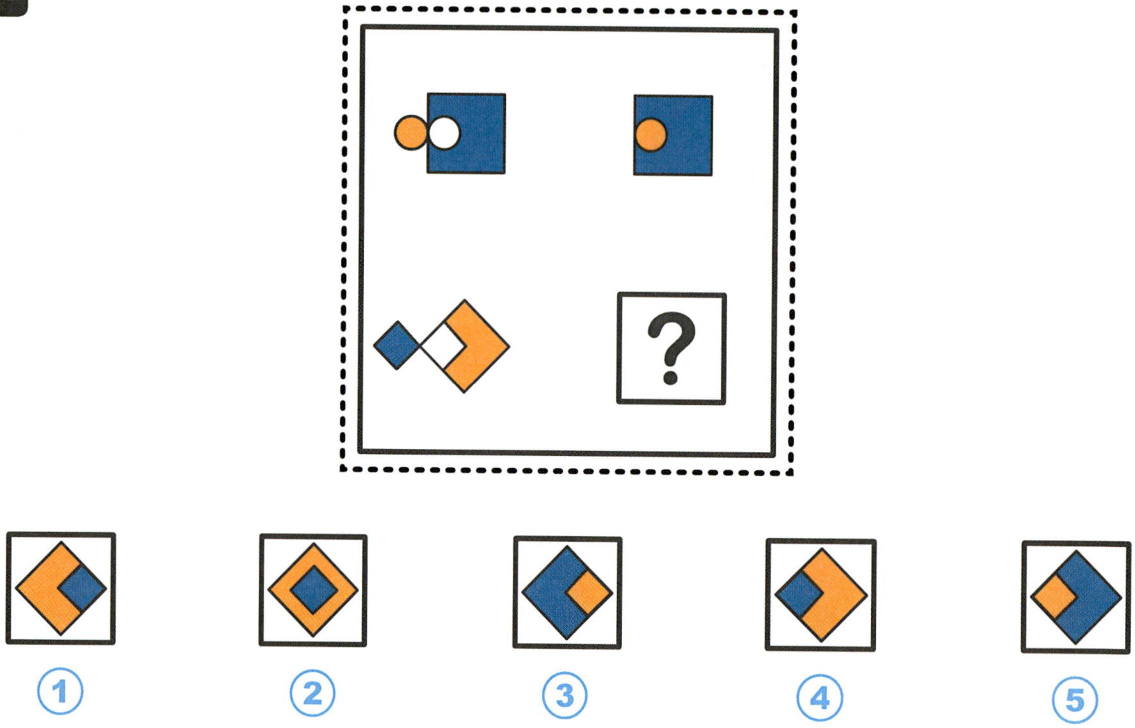

12

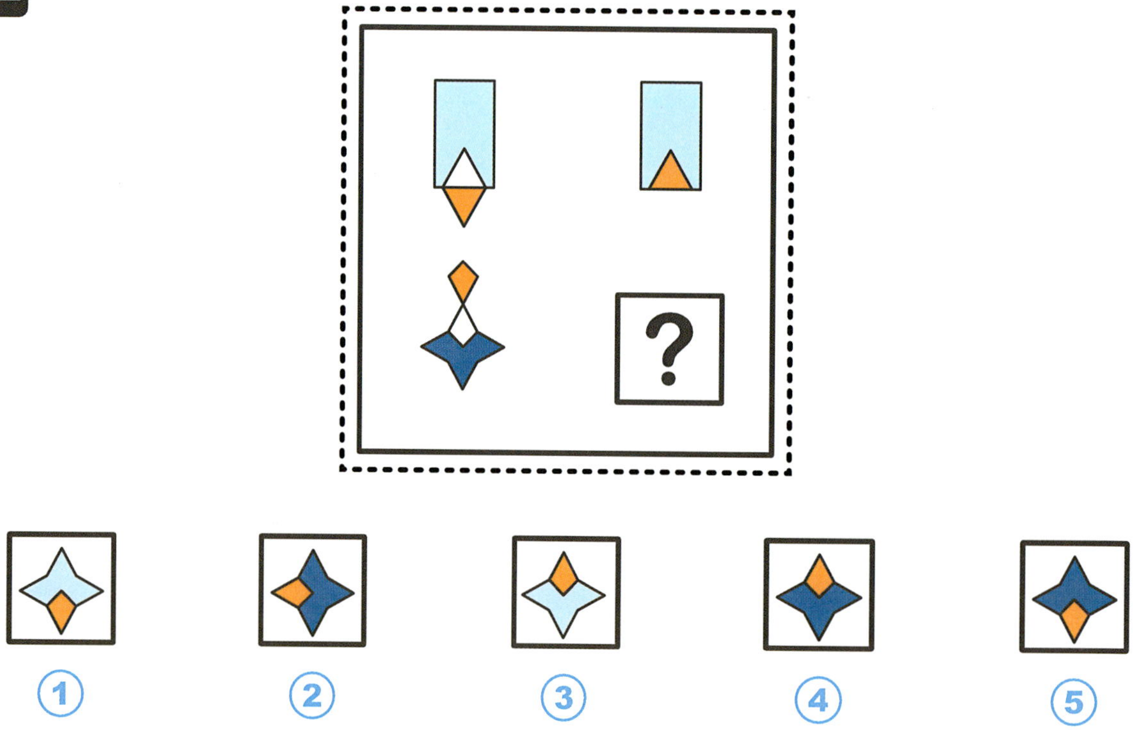

13

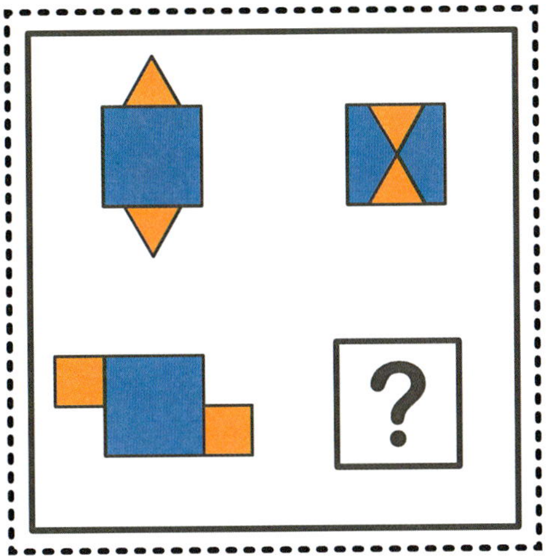

14

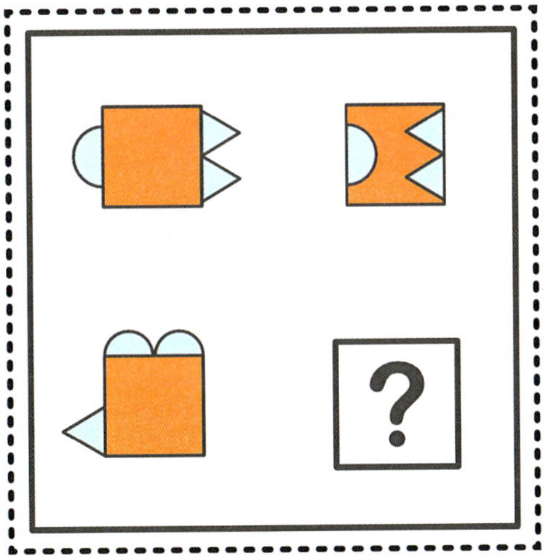

15

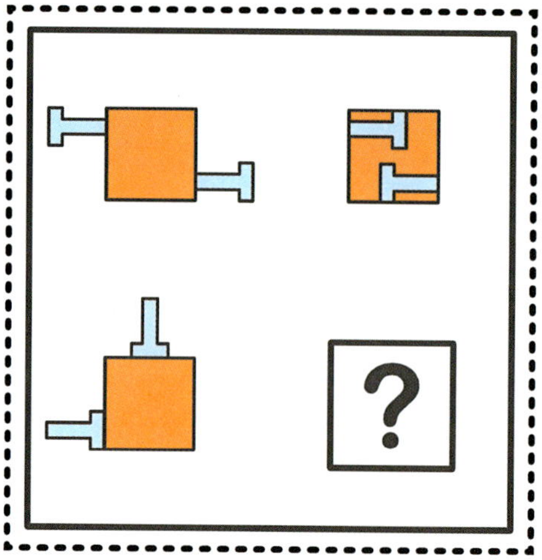

① ② ③ ④ ⑤

16

① ② ③ ④ ⑤

17

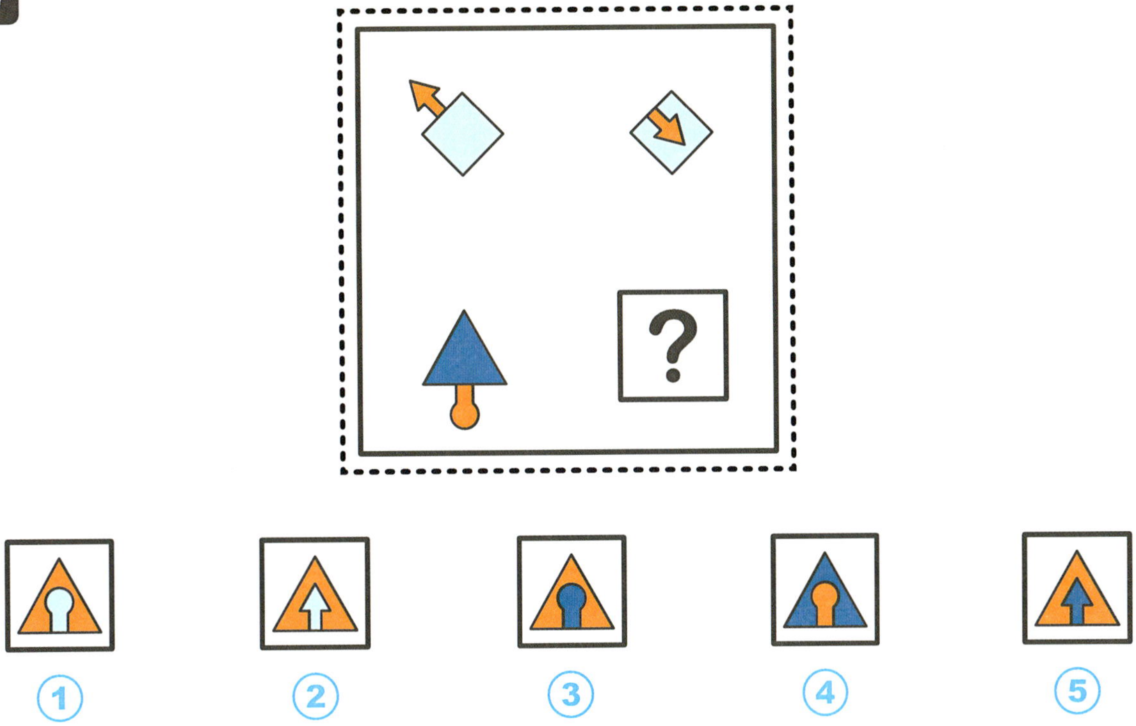

18

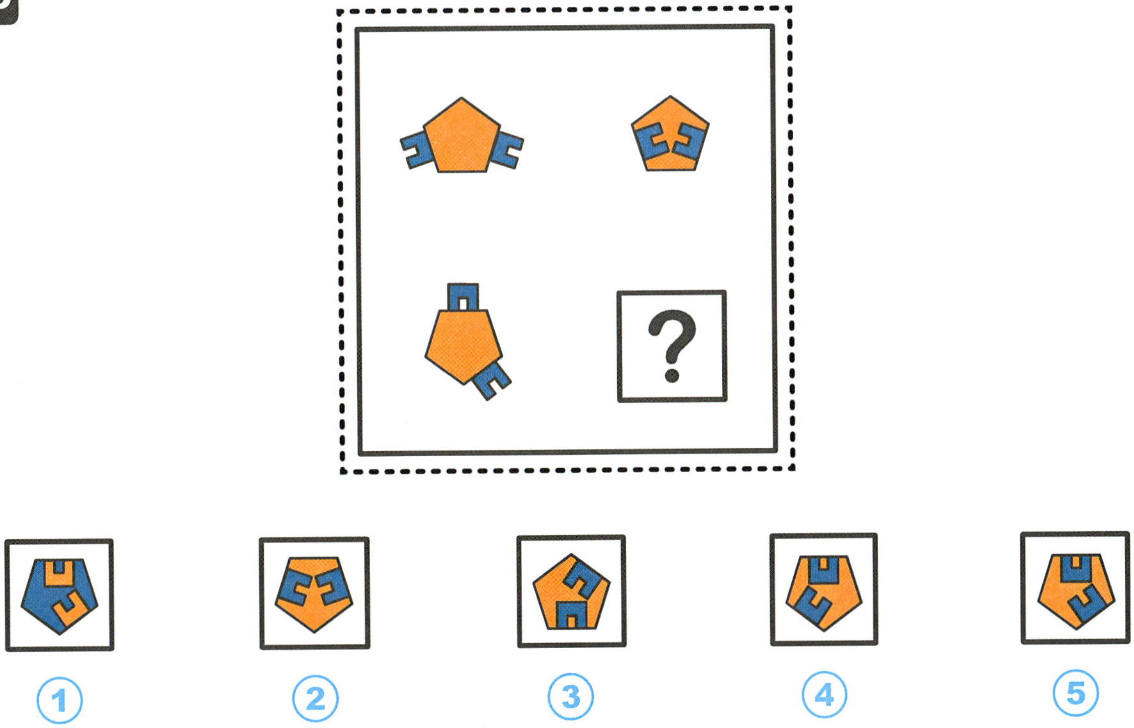

19

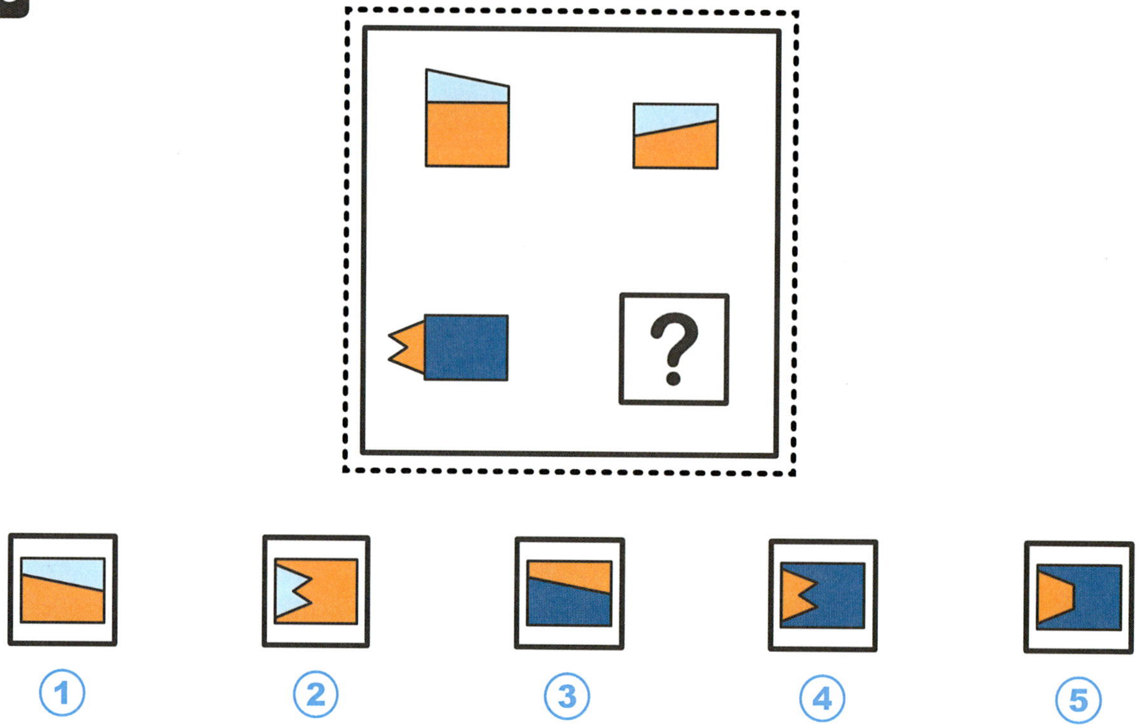

20

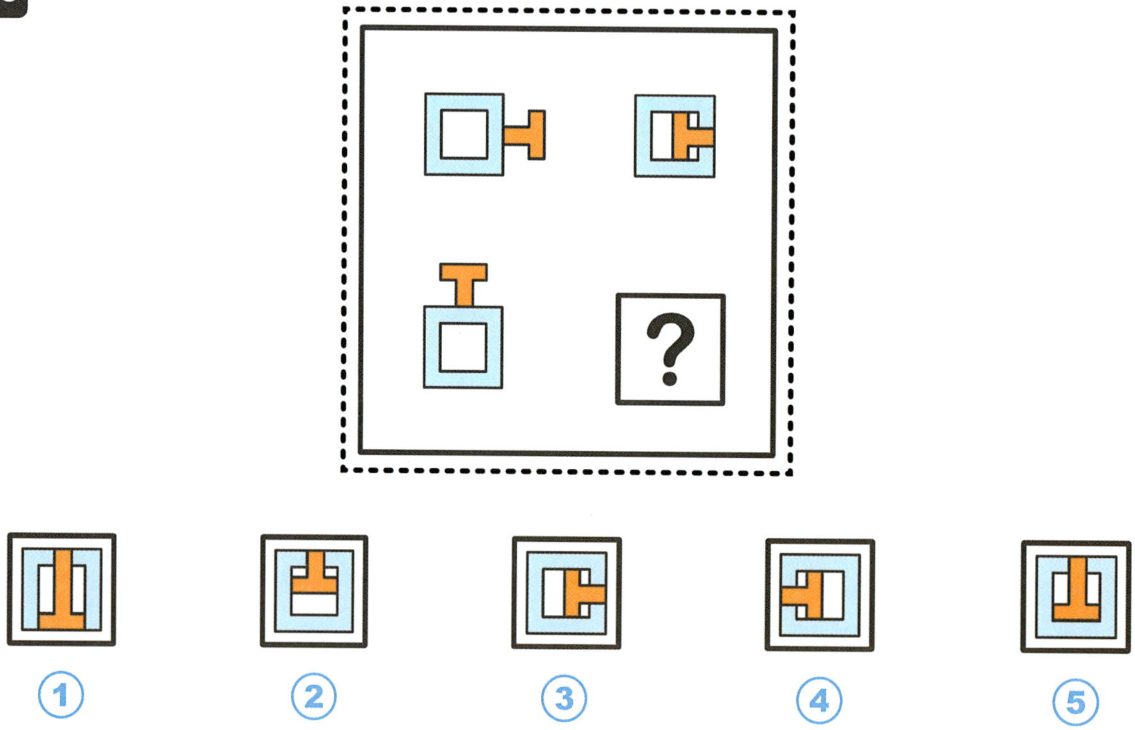

21

1 2 3 4 5

22

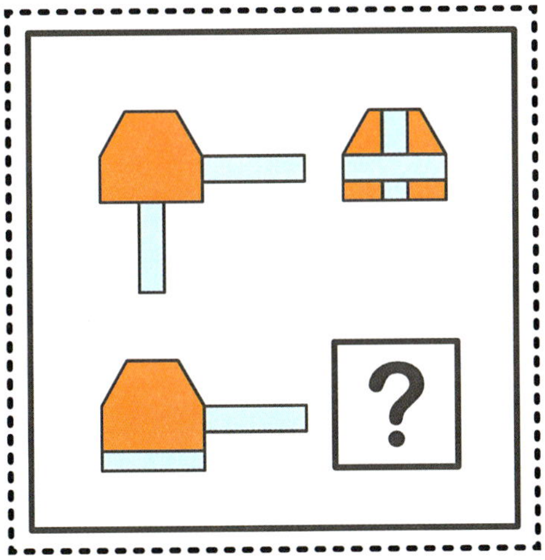

1 2 3 4 5

23

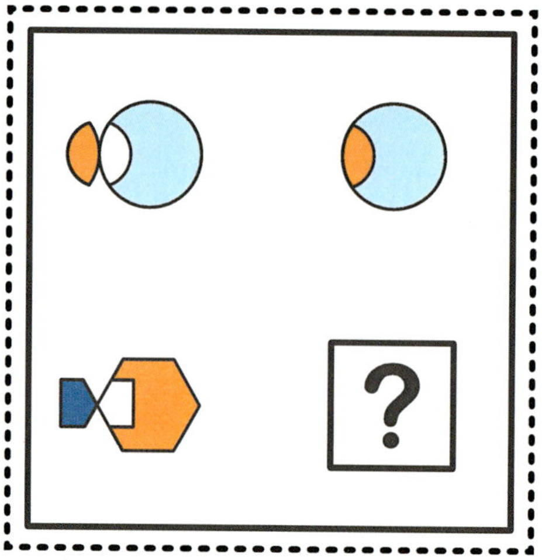

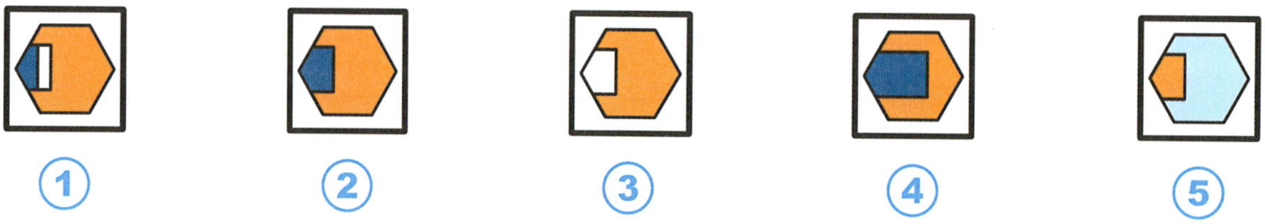

24

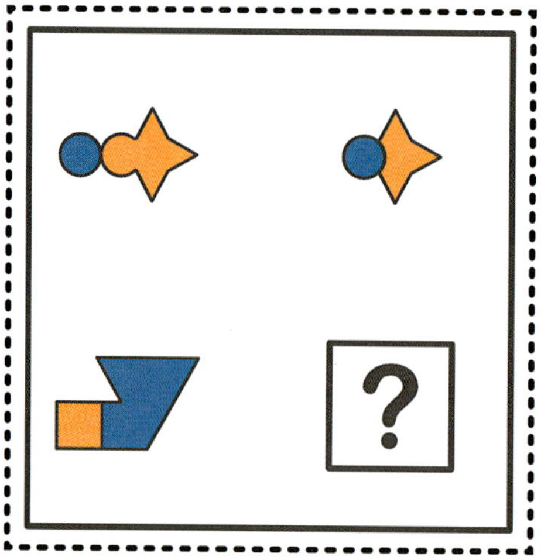

25

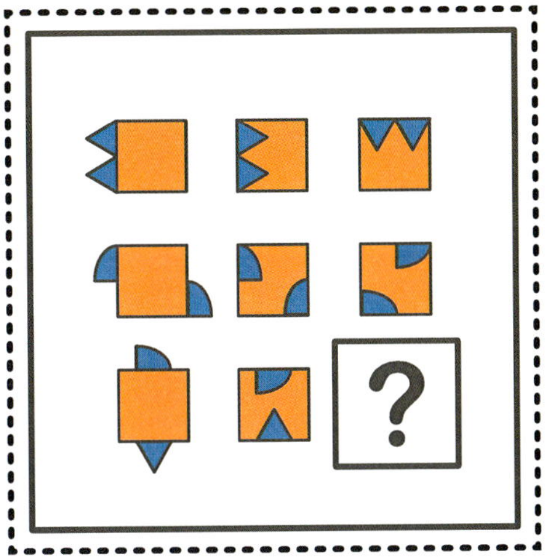

1 2 3 4 5

26

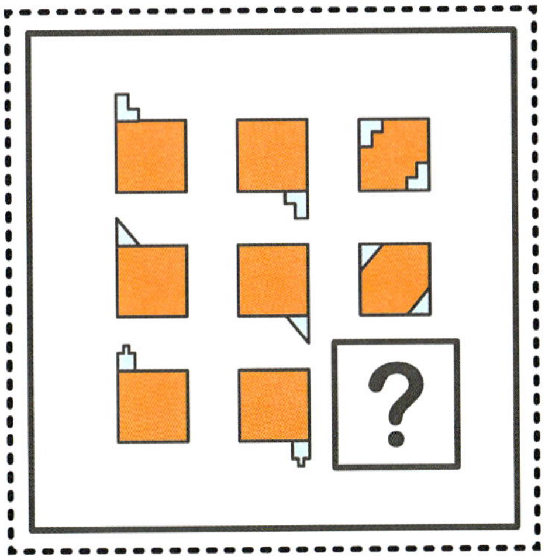

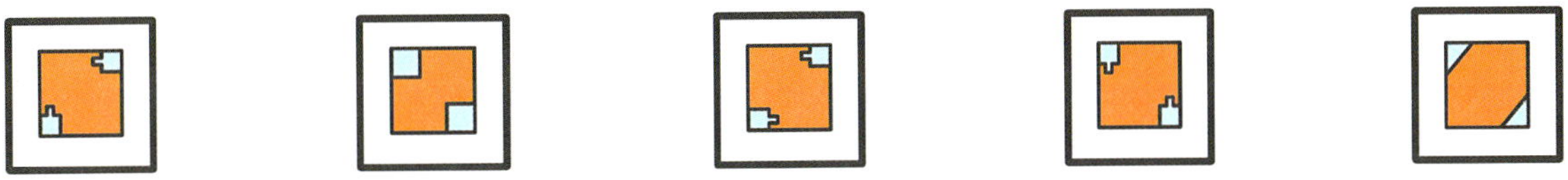

1 2 3 4 5

27

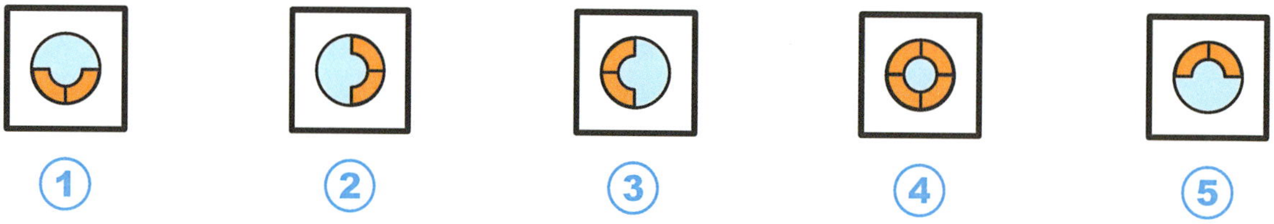

28

29

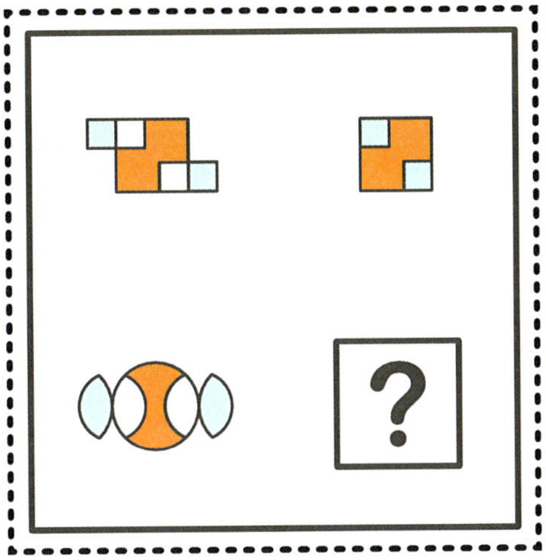

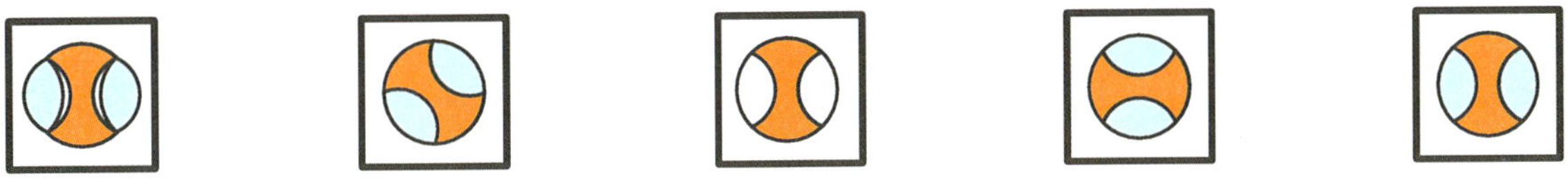

1 2 3 4 5

30

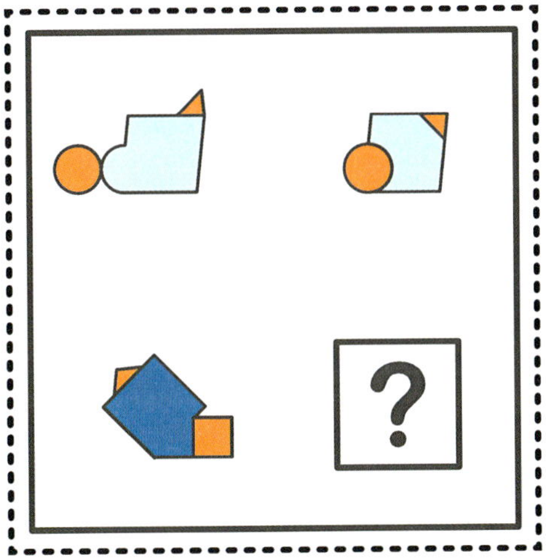

1 2 3 4 5

31

1 2 3 4 5

32

1 2 3 4 5

33

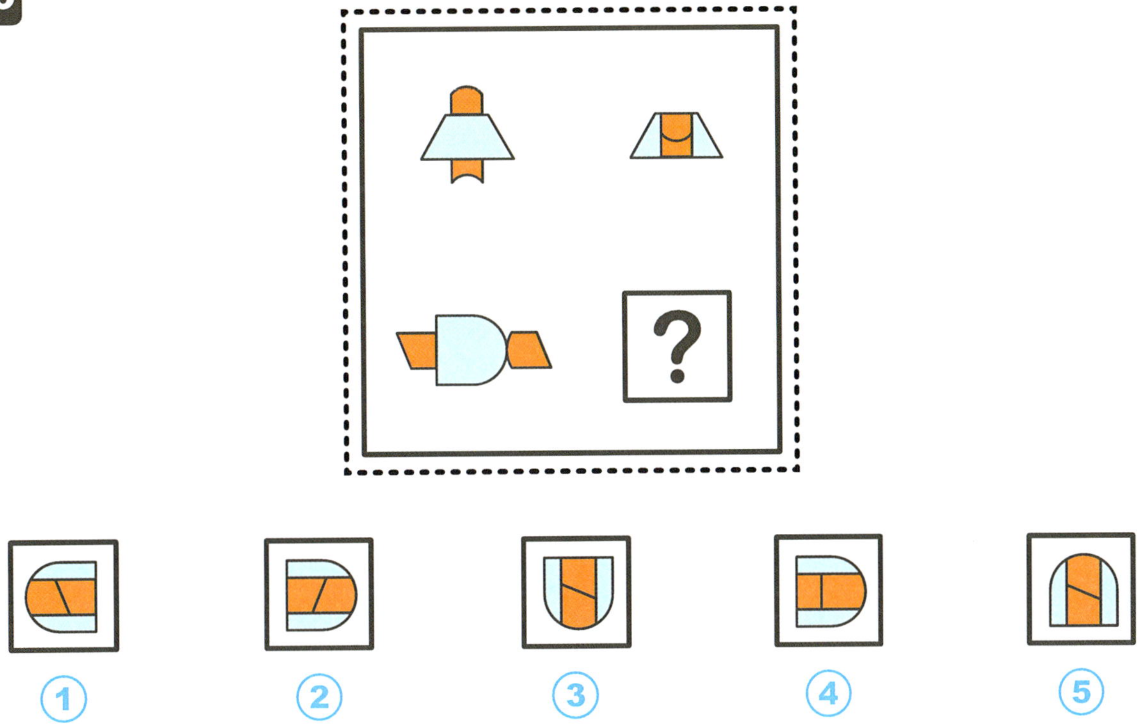

34

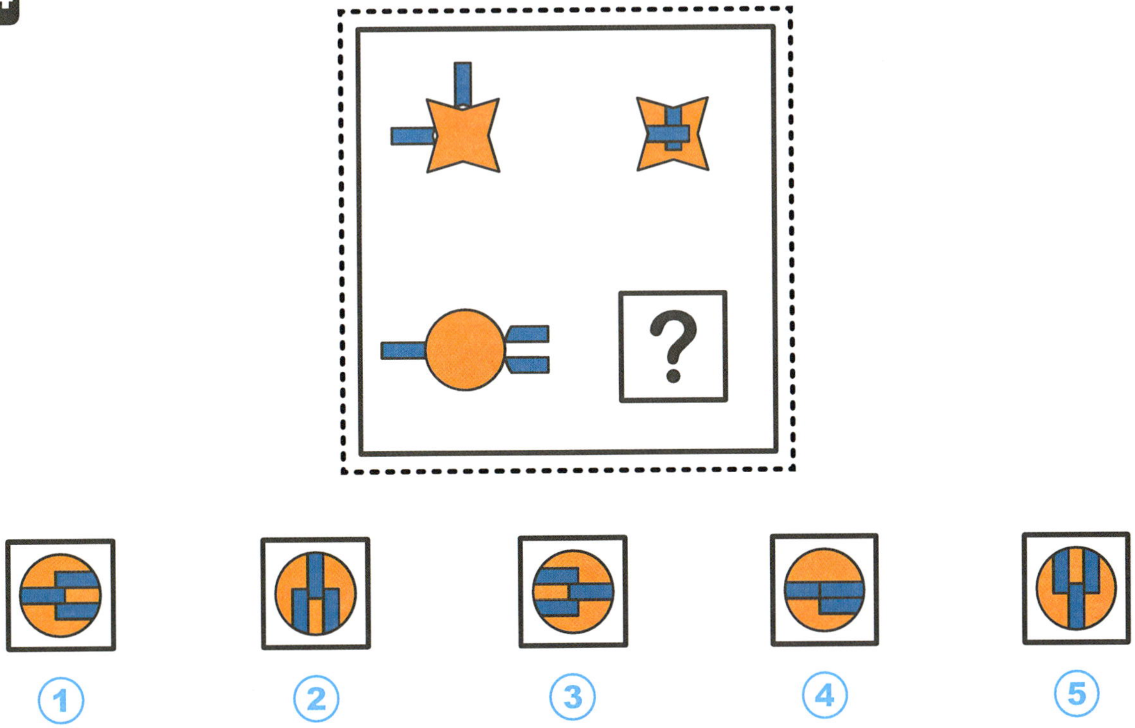

35

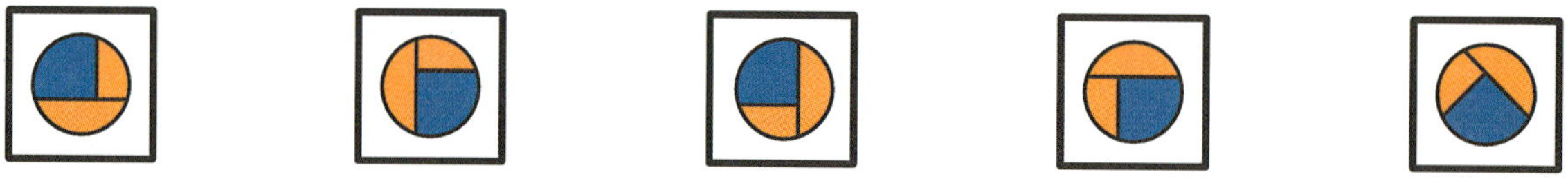

1 2 3 4 5

36

1 2 3 4 5

37

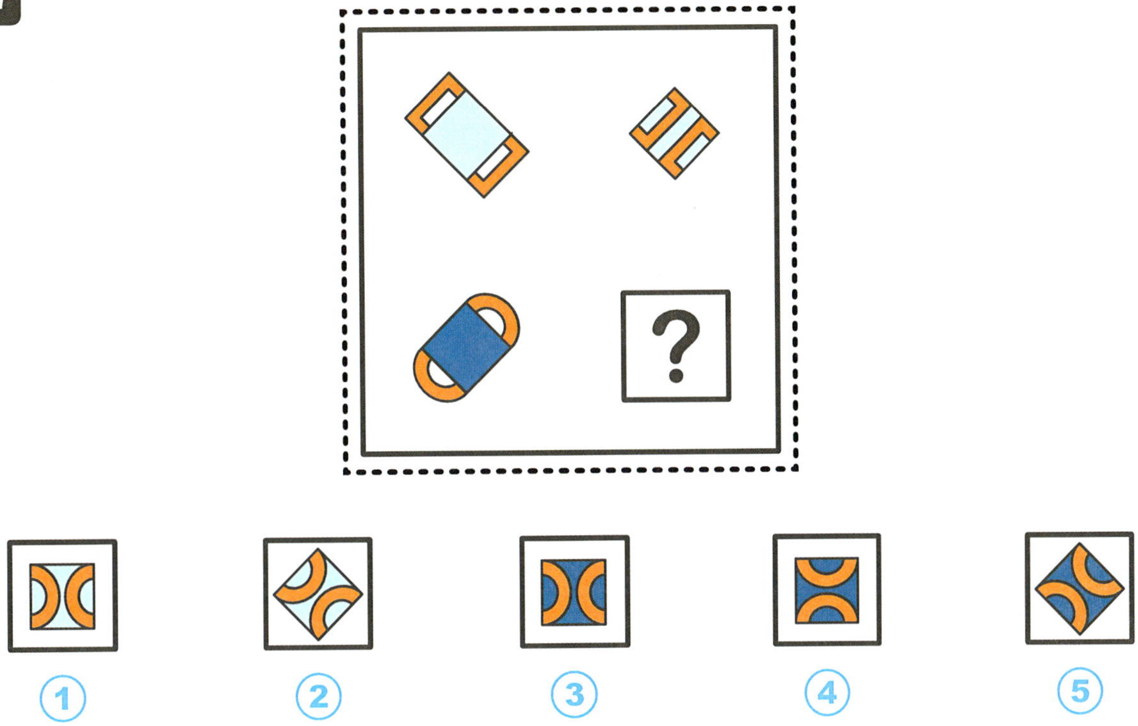

38

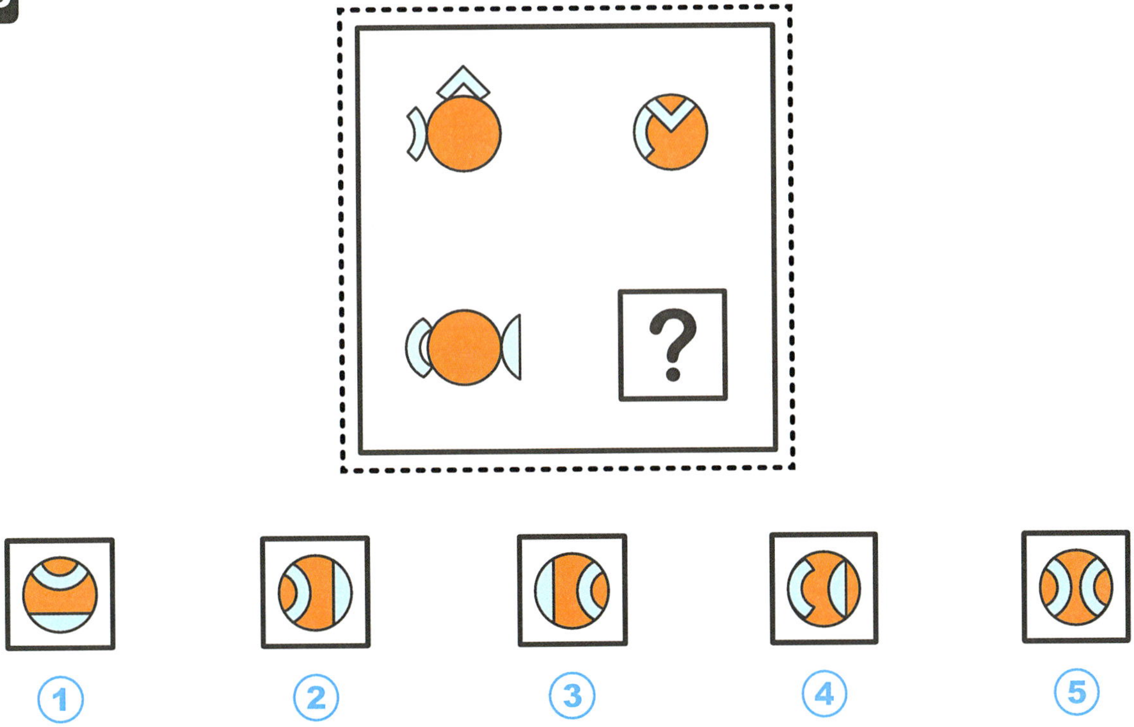

39

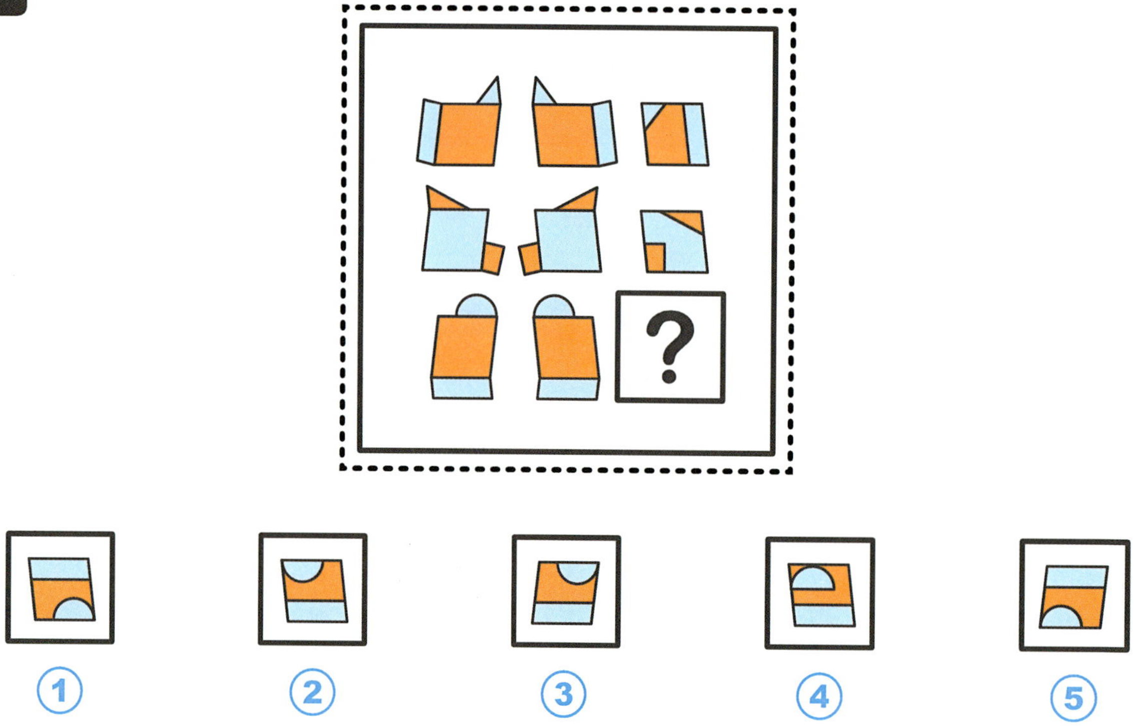

40

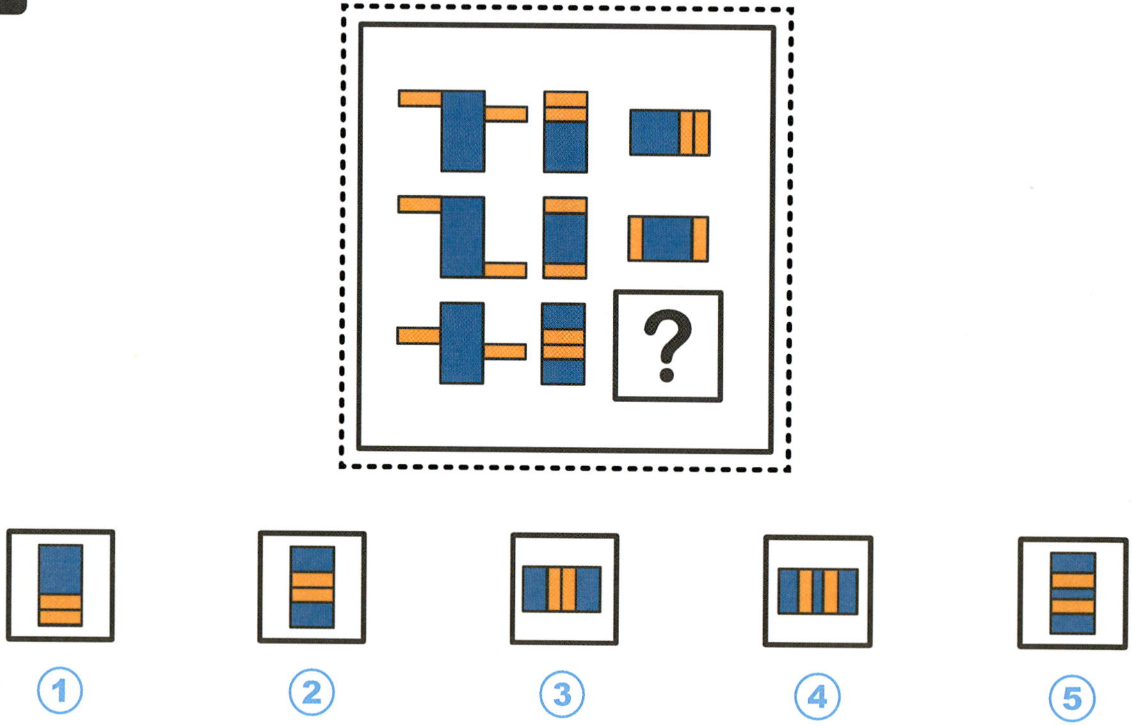

41

42

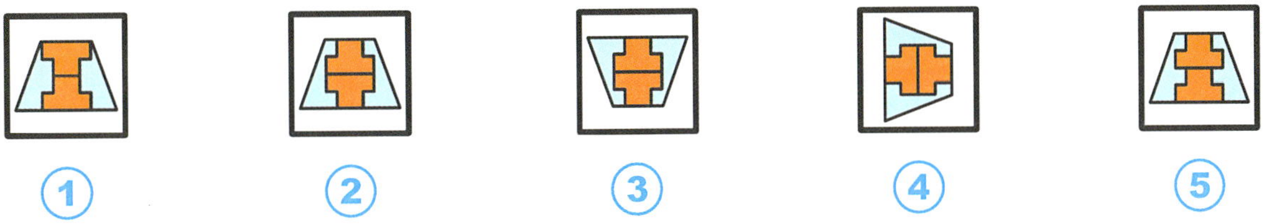

43

1

2

3

4

5

44

1

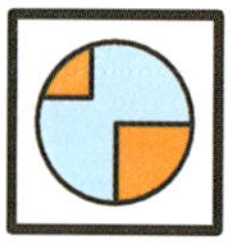

2

3

4

5

45

1

2

3

4

5

46

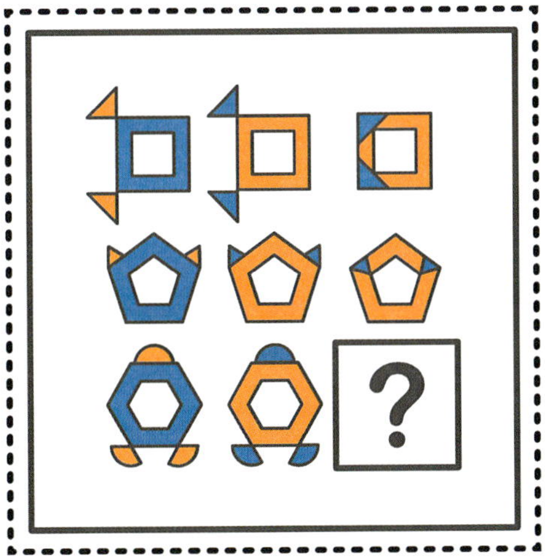

1

2

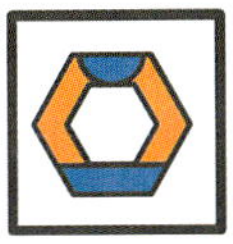
3

4

5

47

1 2 3 4 5

48

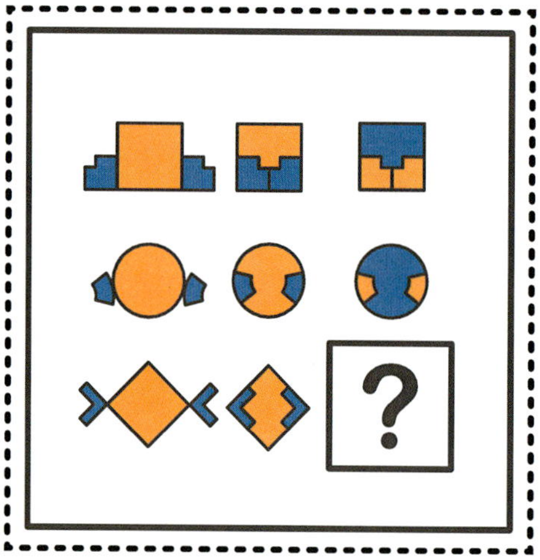

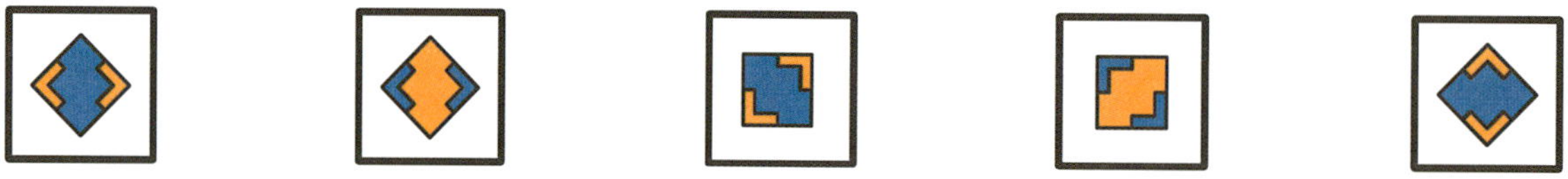

1 2 3 4 5

49

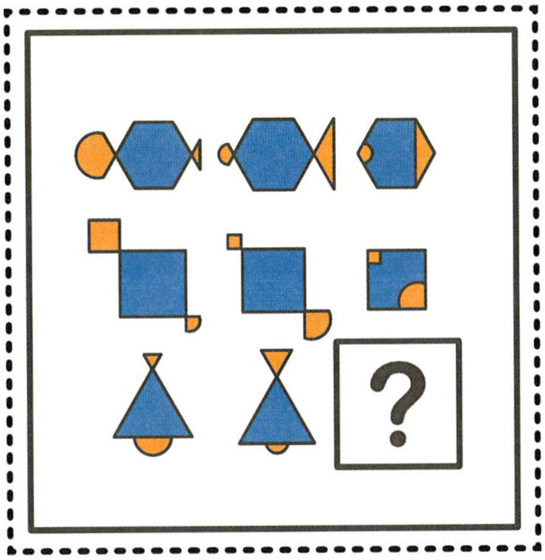

1 2 3 4 5

50

1 2 3 4 5

Bright Kids™ Spatial Visualization Workbook for the NNAT®2

Levels A and B

Additional Challenge:
Paper-Folding Exercises

01

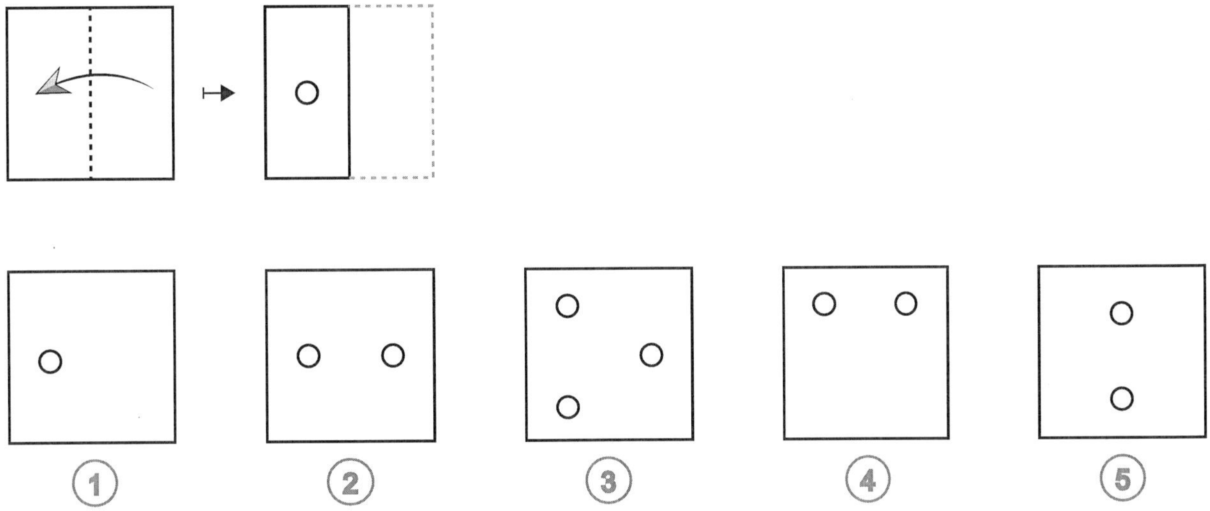

02

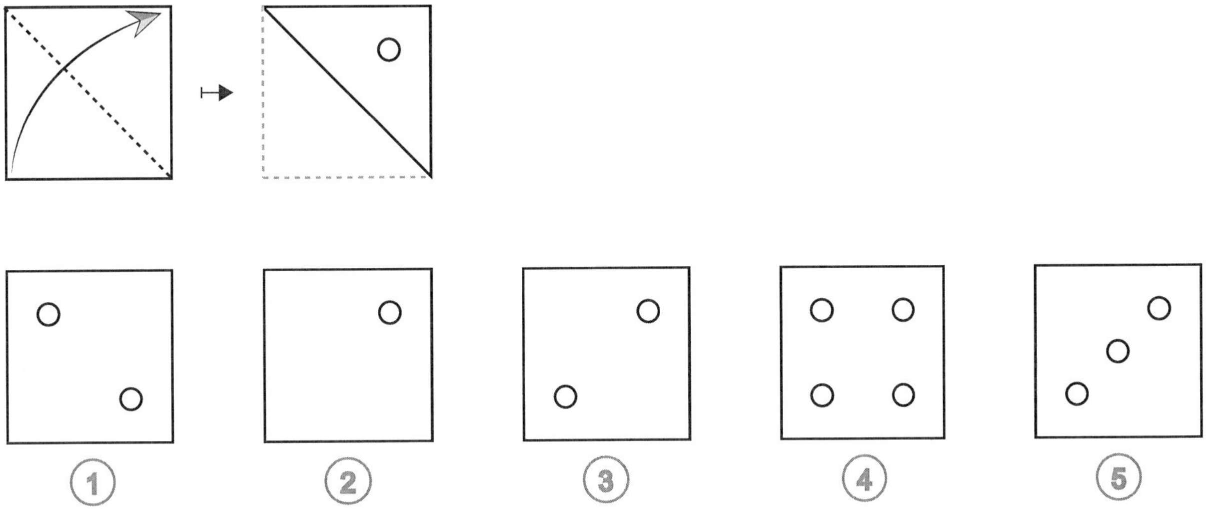

03

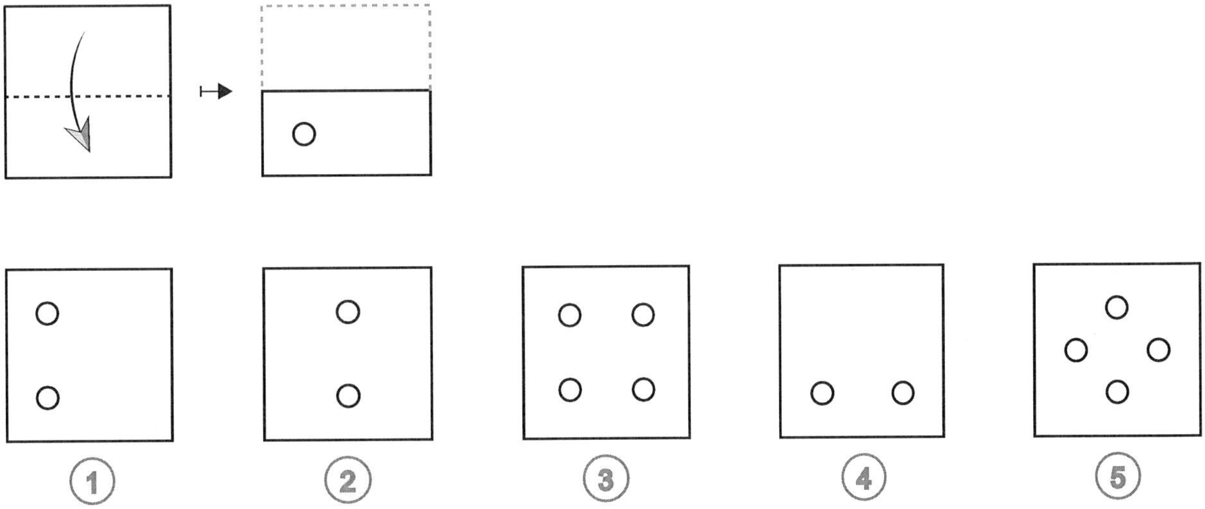

04

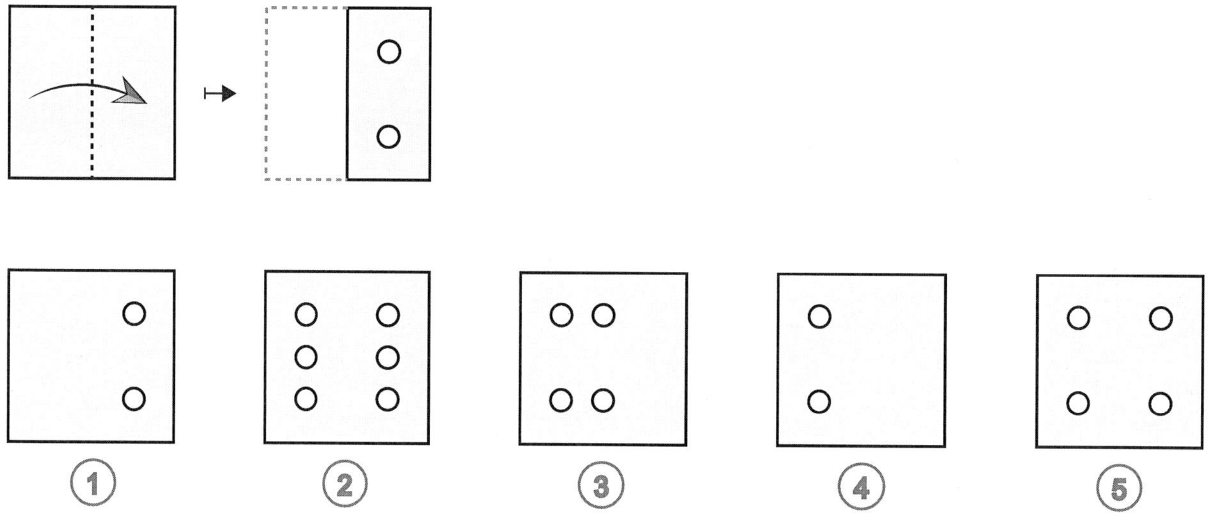

05

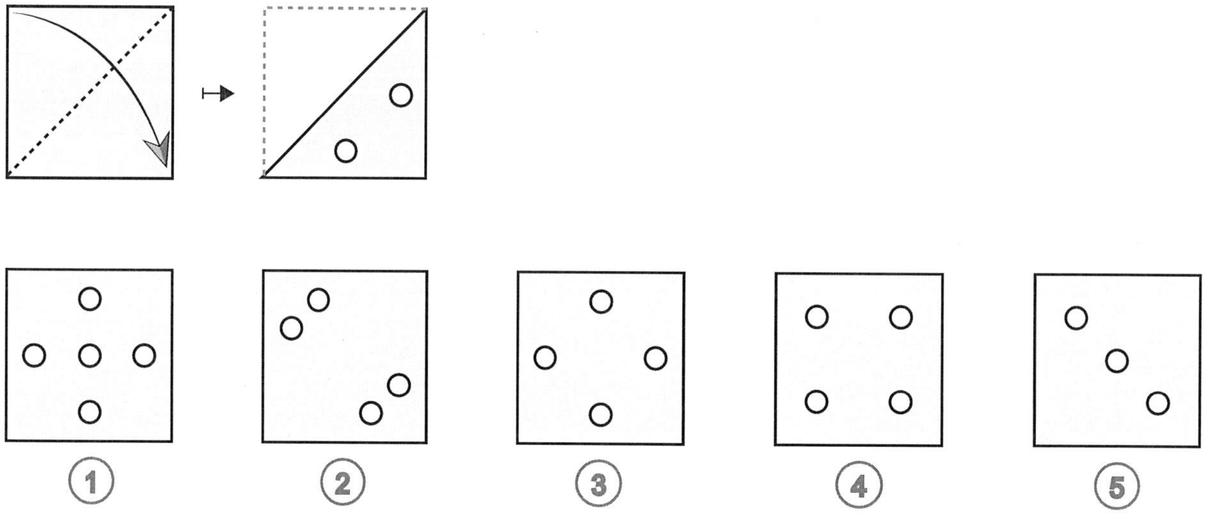

06

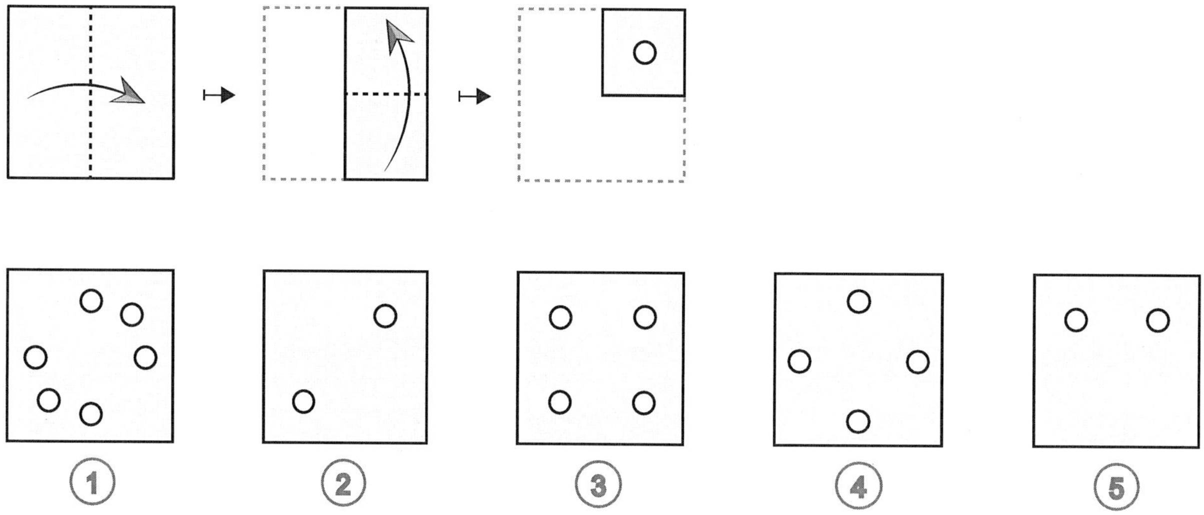

07

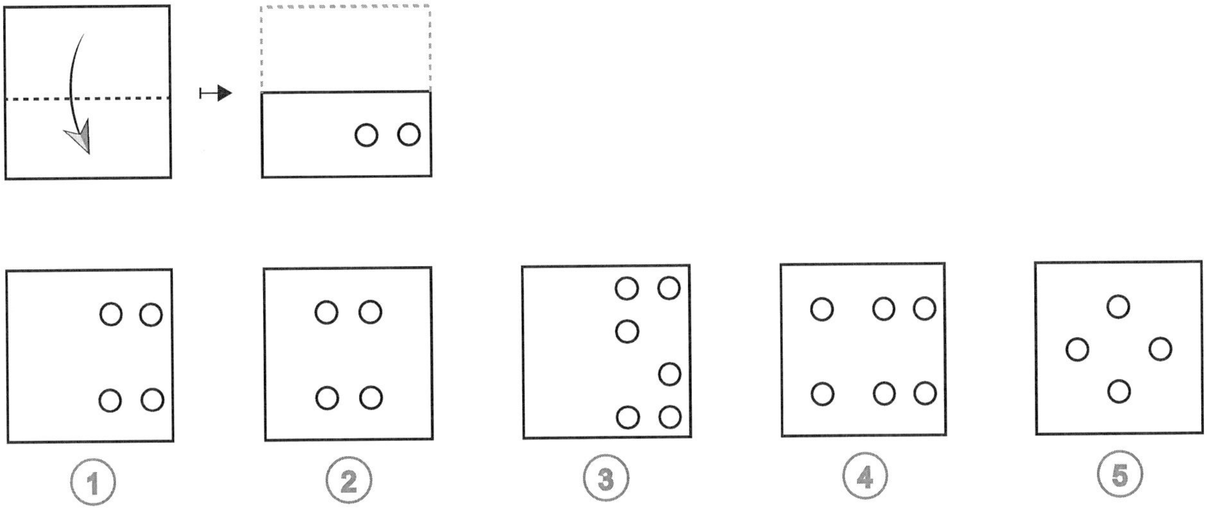

08

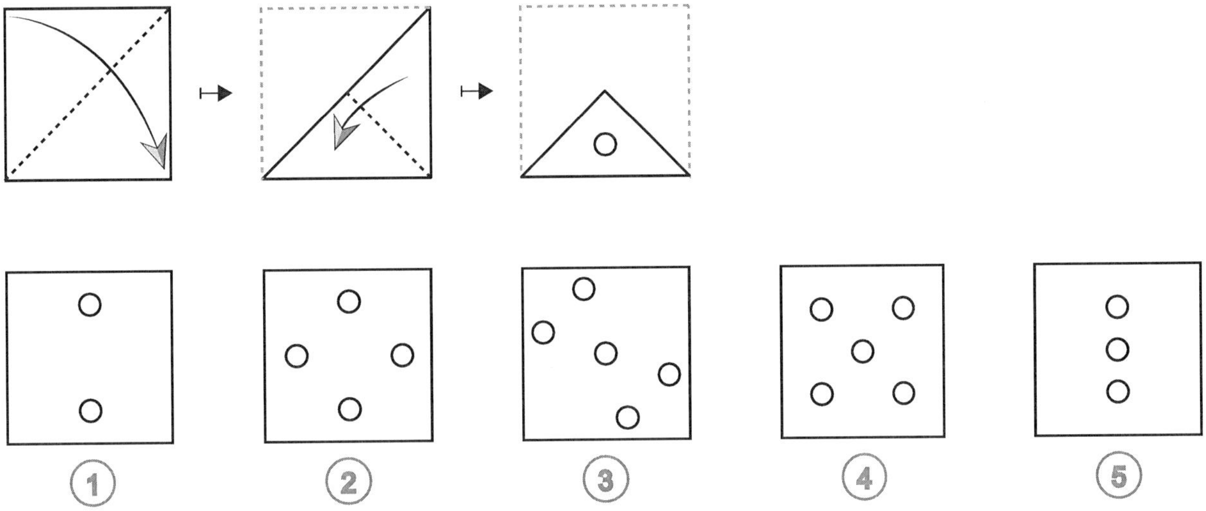

09

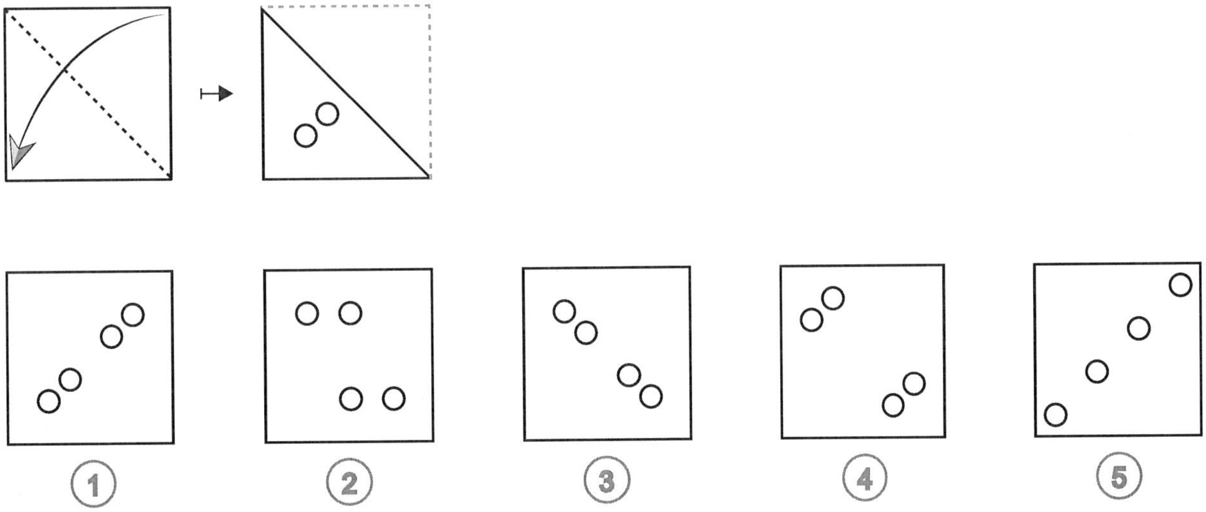

10

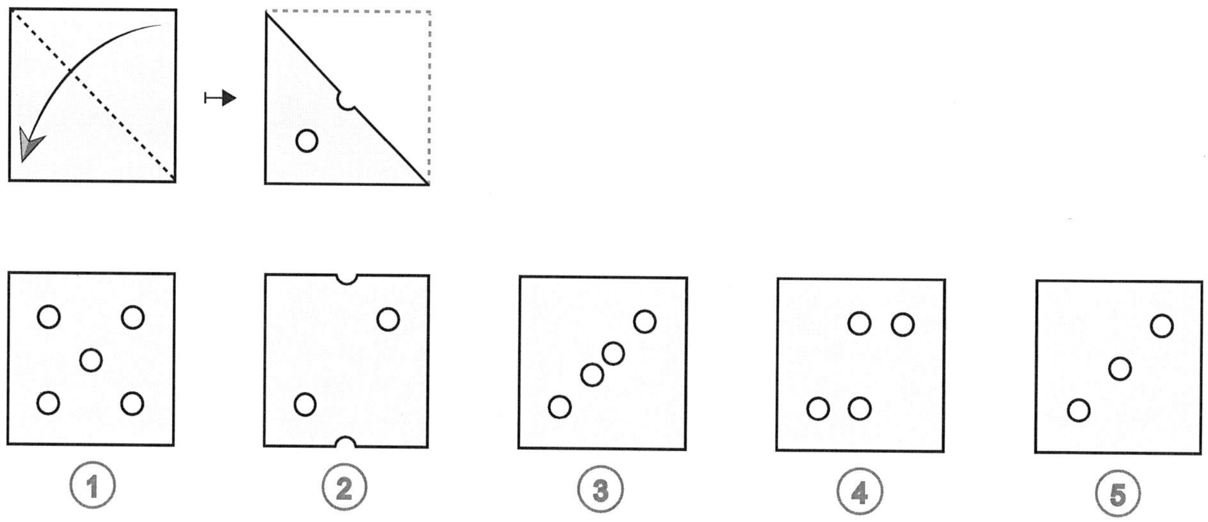

11

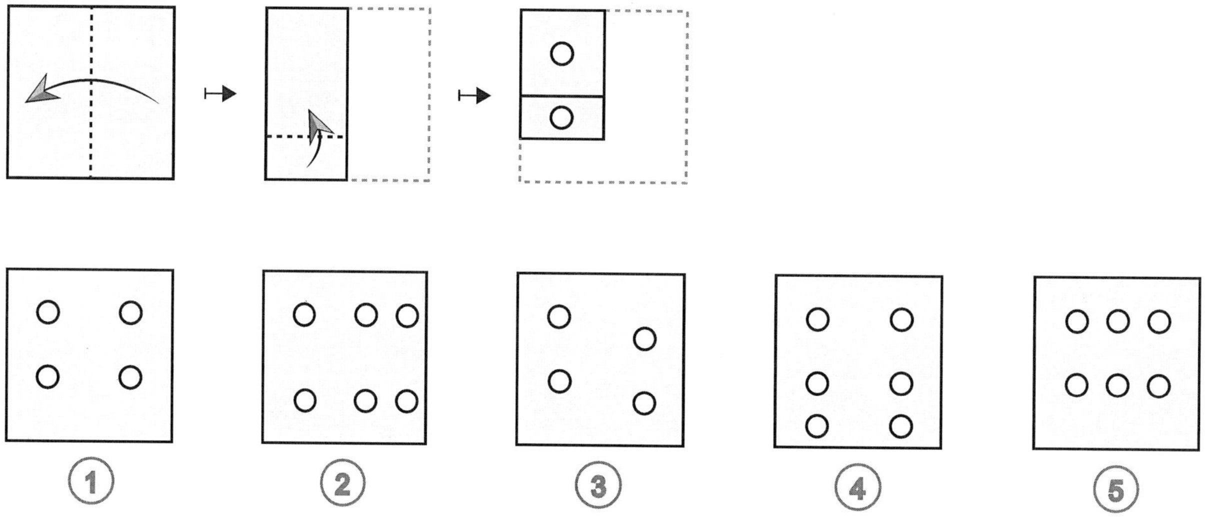

12

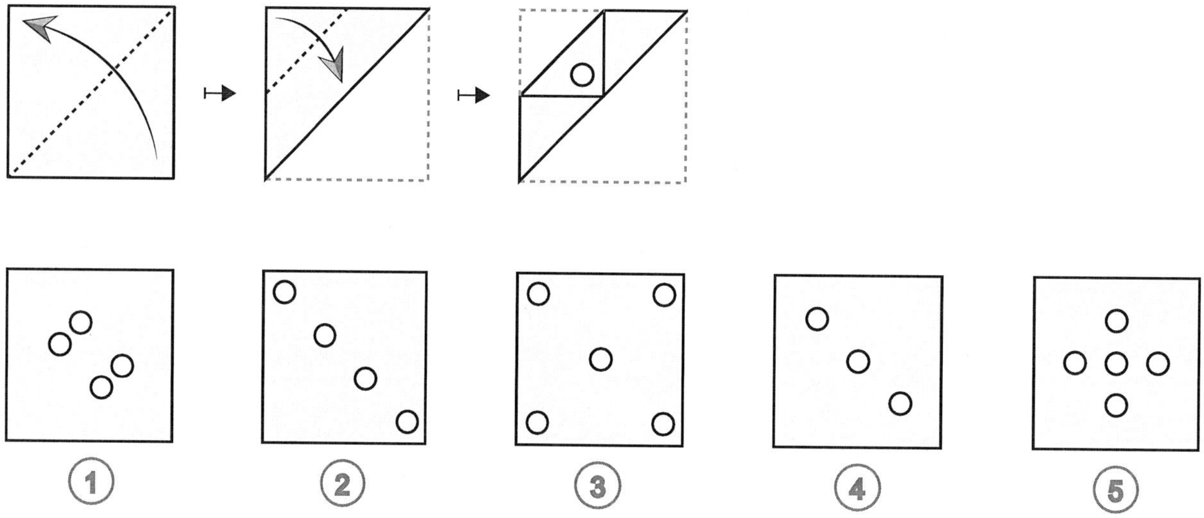

13

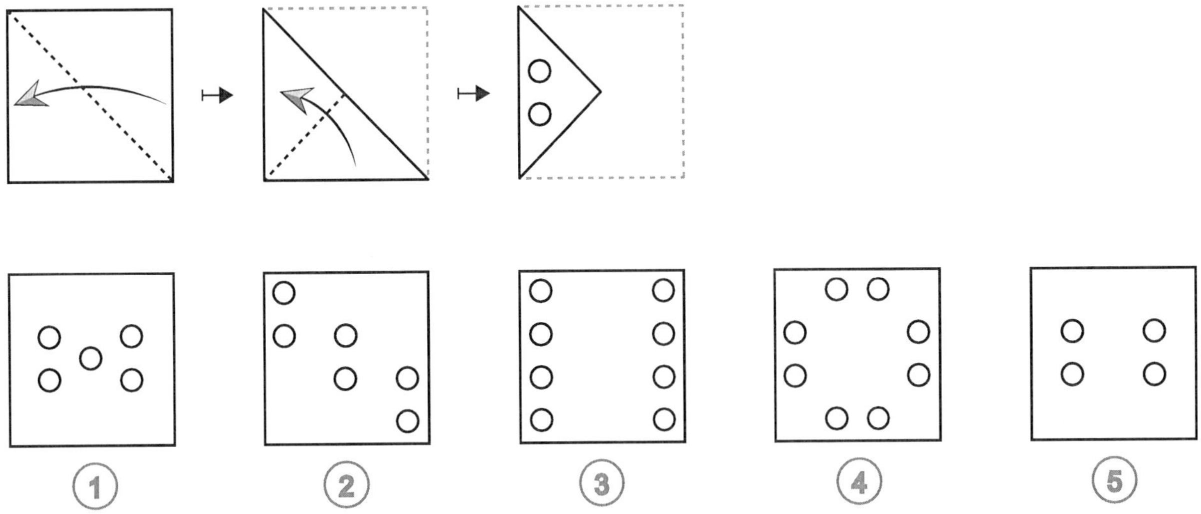

14

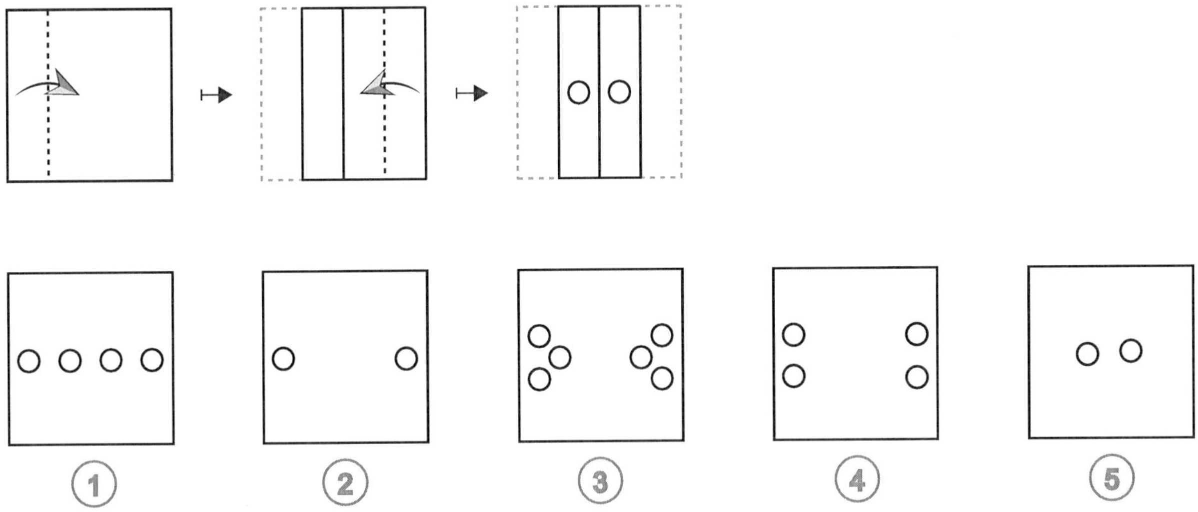

15

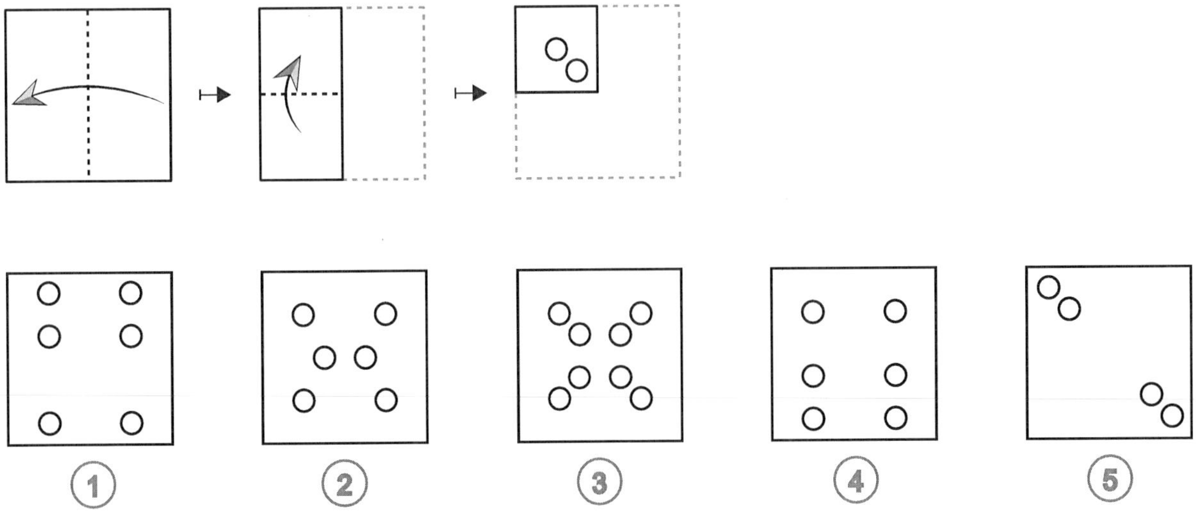

ADDITIONAL CHALLENGE: PAPER-FOLDING EXERCISES

16

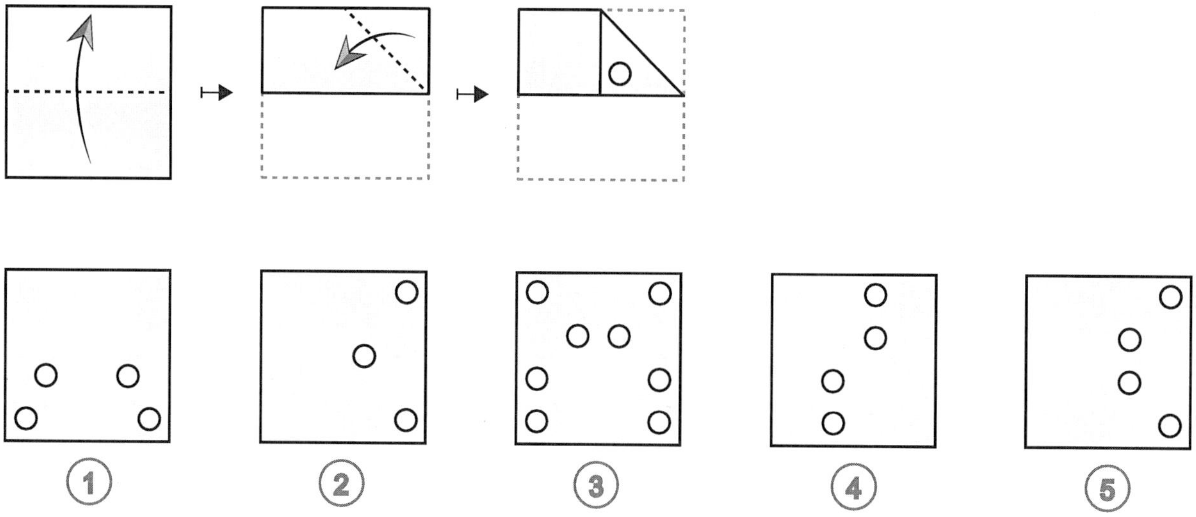

17

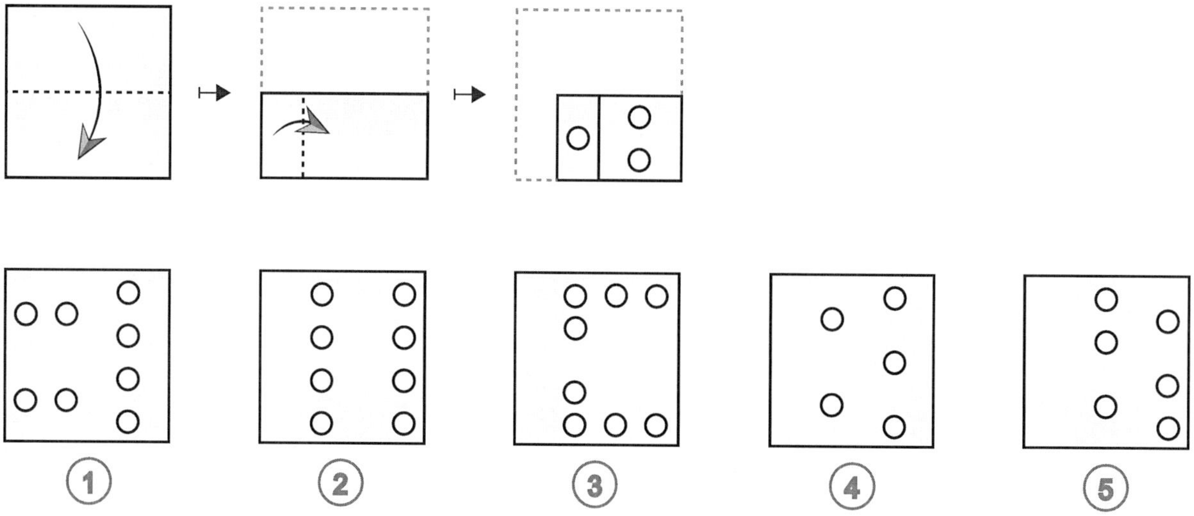

18

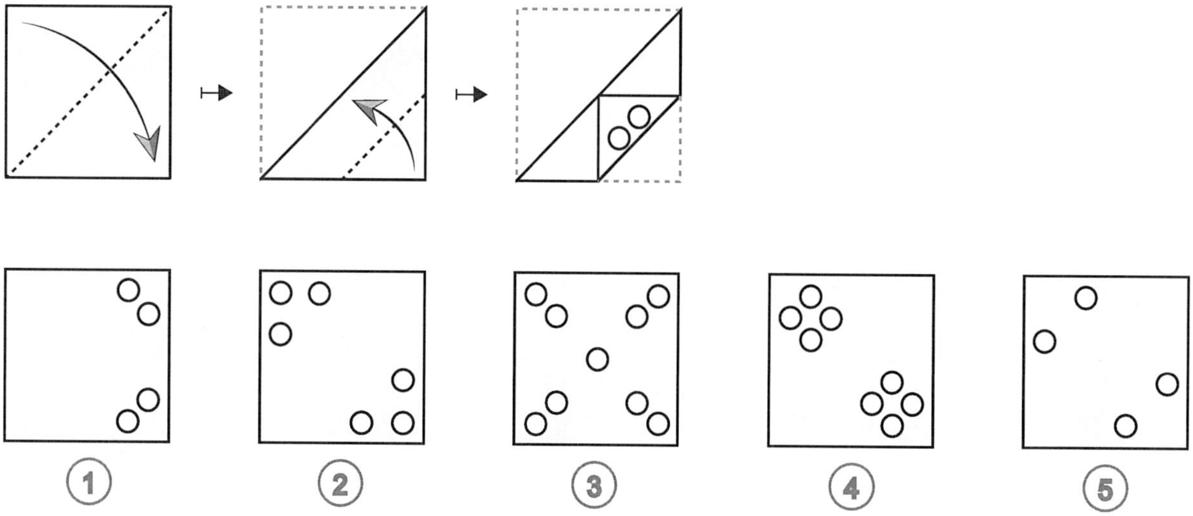

19

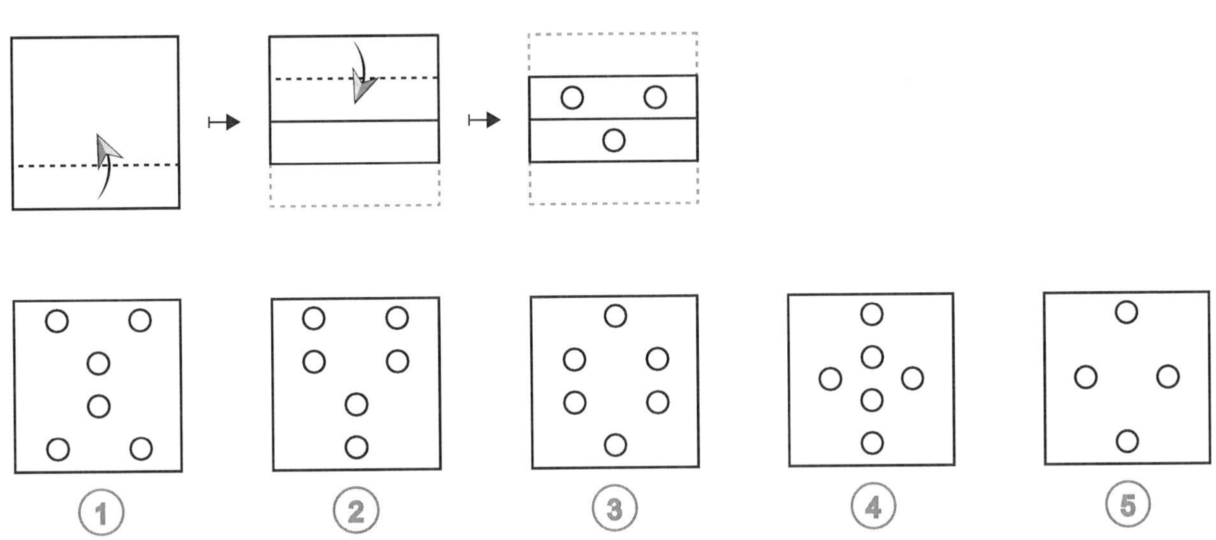

20

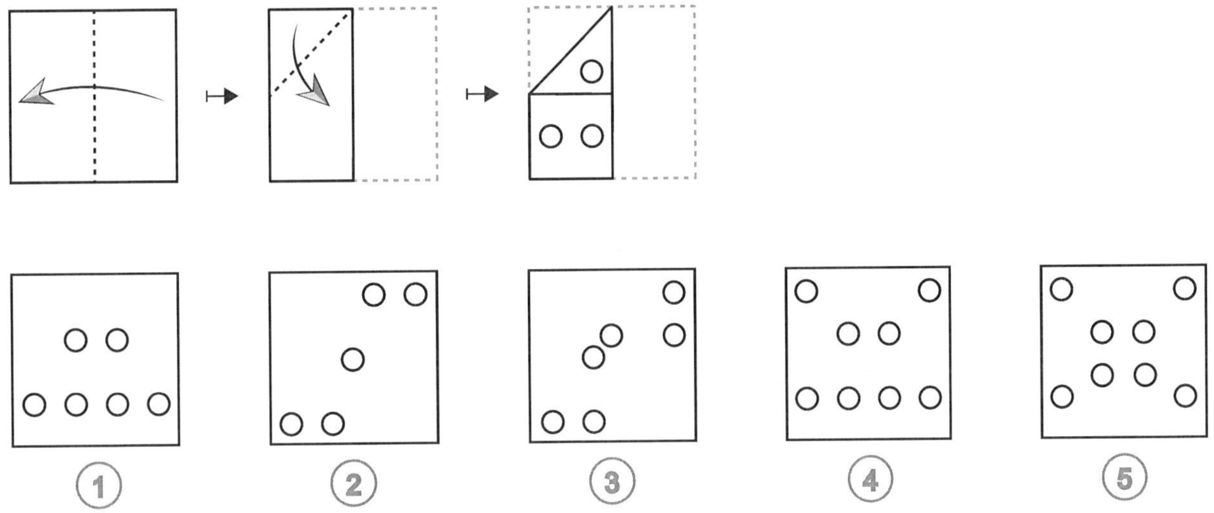

Answer Keys

FIGURAL CONSTRUCTION

	Correct Answer	Child's Answer
1.	1	
2.	3	
3.	2	
4.	4	
5.	3	
6.	3	
7.	1	
8.	4	
9.	1	
10.	3	
11.	4	
12.	4	
13.	1	
14.	3	
15.	4	

	Correct Answer	Child's Answer
16.	3	
17.	2	
18.	1	
19.	3	
20.	4	
21.	3	
22.	2	
23.	1	
24.	4	
25.	3	
26.	2	
27.	3	
28.	1	
29.	1	
30.	4	

FIGURAL DECONSTRUCTION

	Correct Answer	Child's Answer
1.	1,4	
2.	2,3	
3.	1,3	
4.	1,4	
5.	2,3	
6.	1,4	
7.	1,3	
8.	1,2	
9.	2,3	
10.	1,3	
11.	1,2	
12.	3,4	
13.	1,4	
14.	1,3	
15.	2,3	

	Correct Answer	Child's Answer
16.	1,3	
17.	2,3	
18.	1,2	
19.	1,4	
20.	1,4	
21.	1,3	
22.	2,4	
23.	2,3	
24.	1,4	
25.	3,4	
26.	2,3	
27.	1,3	
28.	2,4	
29.	1,4	
30.	1,2	

SPATIAL VISUALIZATION

	Correct Answer	Child's Answer
1.	3	
2.	5	
3.	4	
4.	1	
5.	4	
6.	2	
7.	3	
8.	5	
9.	1	
10.	2	
11.	4	
12.	4	
13.	3	
14.	5	
15.	2	
16.	1	
17.	4	
18.	5	
19.	4	
20.	2	
21.	1	
22.	1	
23.	2	
24.	3	
25.	5	

	Correct Answer	Child's Answer
26.	4	
27.	1	
28.	4	
29.	5	
30.	3	
31.	2	
32.	5	
33.	2	
34.	1	
35.	3	
36.	1	
37.	5	
38.	2	
39.	2	
40.	3	
41.	2	
42.	2	
43.	4	
44.	1	
45.	2	
46.	4	
47.	2	
48.	1	
49.	3	
50.	4	

PAPER-FOLDING EXERCISES

	Correct Answer	Child's Answer
1.	2	
2.	3	
3.	1	
4.	5	
5.	3	
6.	3	
7.	1	
8.	2	
9.	1	
10.	5	
11.	4	
12.	2	
13.	4	
14.	1	
15.	3	
16.	5	
17.	1	
18.	4	
19.	2	
20.	4	